THE EXPERIENCE AND LANGUAGE OF GRACE

The Experience
and
Language of Grace

by
Roger Haight, S.J.

PAULIST PRESS
New York/Ramsey/Toronto

Library of Congress
Catalog Card Number: 79-84403

ISBN: 0-8091-2200-6

Published by Paulist Press
Editorial Office: 1865 Broadway, New York, N.Y. 10023
Business Office: 545 Island Road, Ramsey, N.J. 07446

Printed and bound in the
United States of America

Contents

Preface 1

1. The Experience and Language of Grace 6

2. Augustine: Grace and Human Autonomy 32

3. Aquinas: Nature and Grace 54

4. Luther: Sin and Grace 79

5. Trent: Grace and Justification 105

6. Rahner: Grace and History 119

7. Liberation: A Contemporary Language of Graced
   Experience 143

8. Social Grace: A Liberationist Theology of History 161

Preface

During the academic year 1973-1974 and again in 1974-1975 I had the occasion to teach a basic course on the subject of the theology of grace at Loyola School of Theology in the Philippines. The course I offered consisted of a very close reading by the students and myself of certain fundamental texts from the history of the theology of grace and a thorough discussion of them. Whatever lecturing I did treated the historical and cultural background of the authors and an introduction to their lives and their particular theological language. The authors chosen were Augustine; Thomas Aquinas; Martin Luther, along with the response of the Council of Trent to Luther; and Karl Rahner.[1] As an introduction to the course students read carefully William James's *The Varieties of Religious Experience.*

In preparing this course I found that there was nowhere available one introductory text that adequately surveyed the historical landmarks in the theology of grace, not, at least, for the purposes I had in mind. Where such surveys did exist, they seemed overly abstract in their effort to distill or isolate in propositional form the doctrine of grace from the lives of its proponents and their culture. It goes without saying that the Scholastic systematic presentations of the doctrine of grace were totally inadequate. These essays in the theology of grace, therefore, are an attempt to respond to this need. They are introductory essays and the book is meant for readers approaching the theology of grace for the first time. Although in fact they were addressed to students who already possessed a familiarity with the writings of the several authors they treat, still that background is not necessary for an intelligent appreciation of them. In each case I have tried to summarize the main points from each of these theologians that have flowed into the Western doctrinal tradition.

For a Westerner, teaching theology in non-Western lands today, especially if one lacks a thorough grounding in some form of area studies, is very tricky business. In places like the Philippines there is a very strong demand and need for an indigenous theology. This task requires an appreciation and reformulation of basic Christian doctrines from within the patterns of perception and religious sensibility of a people, in terms of the categories of value and meaning of that particular culture, and corresponding to the ethical exigencies and moral imperatives of the particular situation and society. It is precisely a response to these primary demands that, ordinarily, a Western theologian cannot supply.

What I believe a Western theologian can do in such a situation, however, is to teach history. If this is done with integrity, history will not only introduce those students who study it to the tradition of which they are the direct heirs insofar as they are Christian, but also and at the same time liberate them from that history. This process of relativization, or, better, conscientization I take to be one of the primary values in studying history; it makes one aware of the determinants of the past; it liberates the present for the future.

This problem of inculturation, which is so clear for non-Western Christians today because of the long identification of Christianity with Western culture, is really general and universal. The problem of the relation and adaption of theology to culture, because it exists in its extreme form outside the West, can be seen there with laboratory precision. But actually all theology is an adaptation of Christian faith to culture and there is an equal demand to inculturate the theology of grace into specifically modern and contemporary Western culture in the United States or wherever.

These circumstances and these remarks are meant to explain certain characteristics of this book on the theology of grace. First of all, these essays do not in any way represent an adequate history of the Christian theology of grace, not even within the Western tradition. Not to mention New Testament theology, the teachings of the Greek Fathers with their emphasis on divinization is neglected except insofar as this is retrieved by Aquinas. Practically speaking, the problematic that was begun by Augustine forms the undercurrent of this study and the constructive position that concludes it. Moreover, each of these essays is highly interpretive; they are not meant to set forth a complete account of the theology of a given personality. Also, this interpretation is sometimes set against a contemporary problematic. For example, Augustine's view of grace is set forth over against that of Pelagius because, in a time when human autonomy and its power to direct history is being emphasized, this contrast becomes once again extremely relevant.

Second, there is a deliberate effort to tie the various doctrines of grace to the particular cultural setting and problematic in which it arose as well as to the particular experience of each author. By "experience" I mean more than simply personal experience, although that is also included. The term includes the cultural categories that may mediate experienced meaning. And by "language" I mean more than word symbols. The term includes philosophical or systematic concepts by which meanings are rendered coherent. Thus the terms experience and language are correlative, since all adult experience is linguistic; they merely point to different levels of perception. This emphasis on the particularity of each author's experience and language of grace is meant to stimulate one's own personal experience of the same reality, for one can only perceive the particularity of another's peculiar position against the horizon of one's own appreciation of the matter, either as common with that of the other or as distinct from it, that is, by an experience of either commonality or distinction. Thus, for example, if one appreciates Aquinas's experience and language of grace as both coherent and intelligible on the one hand, and on the other as bizarre relative to one's own way of thinking, one has at the same time experienced both what he is trying to communicate and the freedom to try to express it in a current language.

Third, and similarly, there is also a deliberate effort to stress those aspects in which the several doctrines of grace of the various authors differed and the reasons for this difference and change. Once again, the more deeply one appreciates the differences in the various doctrines of grace through the history of one's own tradition, the more any one of them is relativized and the more free one is to begin to formulate one's experience for the present. But at the same time, seeing the differences in a comparison between two thinkers on the same subject also releases an experience of the fundamental perceptions they share in common. Paradoxically, then, the lines of continuity appear at their most basic and real level when differences are clearly drawn.

One could of course have stressed the other side of each of these coins; primary attention could have been given to the essential Christian core in each thinker and consequently to what they all share in common. Against this background, differences would seem minimal or accidental relative to a common "core" experience. But such a stress, and we are speaking of emphases here, would not have fit my purpose, which is to demonstrate the extent to which historical factors, both personal and cultural, determine doctrine. The hope is that the very perception of this will liberate the reader to search and express his or her own experience, in this case a *docta experientia*, which is the precondition and supposition for a theology that is indigenous to any cultural situation and at the same time continuous with the Christian tradition.

There are many people to whom I am deeply indebted in the preparation of this book. I wish to thank especially, however, the students I had the pleasure of working with at Loyola School of Theology in Quezon City, Philippines, who in their enthusiasm, acceptance and warm friendship stimulated me to write these essays and made my stay there challenging, fruitful and enjoyable. I would also like to thank Ms. Irene Skala of Jesuit School of Theology in Chicago for her dedication in typing the final manuscript.

Chapter 2 of this book originally appeared as "Notes on the Pelagian Controversy" in *Philippine Studies* 22 (1974) and chapter 8 as well as part of chapter 7 appeared as "Salvation, Grace, Liberation: A Liberationist Interpretation of History" in *The Thomist* (1978).

Notes

1. The texts read in the course were the following: Augustine, *Confessions*, Book VIII; "On the Spirit and the Letter," *Basic Writings of Saint Augustine*, I, Whitney Oates, ed. (New York: Random House, 1948); Aquinas, *Summa Theologiae*, vol. 30 (Ia–IIae, QQ. 109–114), Blackfriars Edition (New York: McGraw Hill Book Company, 1972); Martin Luther, "The Freedom of the Christian Man," in *Martin Luther: Selections from His Writ-*

ings, ed. John Dillenberger (Garden City, N.Y.: Anchor Books, Doubleday & Co., 1961); The Council of Trent, "The Decree on Justification," in *The Church Teaches*, ed. and trans. John Clarkson et al. (St. Louis: B. Herder Book Co., 1955); Karl Rahner, "Some Implications of the Scholastic Concept of Uncreated Grace," *Theological Investigations* I (Baltimore: Helicon Press, 1961); "Concerning the Relationship between Nature and Grace," ibid.; "Nature and Grace," *Theological Investigations* IV (Baltimore: Helicon Press, 1966); "Reflections on the Experience of Grace," *Theological Investigations* III (1976); "History of the World and Salvation-History," *Theological Investigations* V (1966); "Christianity and the Non-Christian Religions," ibid.; "Christianity and the 'New Man,'" ibid.

1

The Experience
and Language of Grace

"Grace"

The word "grace" is one of the most common in the Christian vocabulary. At the same time, it is probably the most slippery word to define. Of all Christian terms, the word grace is the simplest, and at the same time it is the most complicated. Grace refers to the most basic and fundamental of Christian realities since it indicates the presupposition of all Christian spirituality. And yet the word has acquired so many different secondary meanings in technical theology, in doctrine and in common understanding, that it is almost impossible to say what exactly the word grace means. In fact, grace means many different things to different Christians; it corresponds to many different Christian experiences and understandings. But in all of them, there should be some inner core that remains the same.

One of the reasons for this ambivalent situation seems to lie in the nature of the word itself. Without being technical, for this is not the point here, the word grace is the English equivalent of the Latin *gratia*, which in turn translates the Greek word *charis*; and the New Testament authors used *charis* "to render several Hebrew words conveying meanings reducible to three main ideas: condescending love, conciliatory compassion and fidelity."[1] As a result, the word grace has the special connotation of everything that pertains to a gift of love; it is totally gratuitous or unmerited and undeserved. Grace is not due to any right on the part of human beings and God is wholly free in bestowing it. This is one characteristic of grace that is common to all understanding of it.

But when the further question of "Giving what?" arises, so also does the problem. For the word grace, although a substantive in form, has for all practical purposes an adjectival meaning—it is the gratuitous quality of God's special love for people. And because of this adjectival usage, the word grace can literally apply to everything in the Christian dispensation. Christ is God's grace to human existence and so is his Spirit. What Christ did for us—redemption; what he gained for us—salvation; and the fact that this has been made known—revelation; all of these mysteries are grace.

Thus it appears that within the Christian dispensation the word grace in its root sense does not have any specific content of its own. That is to say, it applies at once to the whole Christian economy and to any single mystery within that economy. It can be used to designate that by which God heals us, forgives us, elevates us; it is at once the Holy Spirit and the New Creation of the Holy Spirit; grace is Christ himself and Christ working within the Christian; all Christian mysteries share in the gratuitous quality of the love of God by which he bestowed them on humanity. Therefore the primary objective sense of grace is really found in all of the fundamental areas of Christian theology, in the theology of Christ, of revelation, of faith, of the Holy Spirit, of the sacraments. But on the other hand, the word grace is still a substantive and has a matter of fact been used substantively in the Christian vocabulary. And as such, it has been defined in a myriad of different contexts and problematics throughout Christian history. Thus the concrete or direct denotation of the word grace can only be unraveled by a long study of history. And that history has so twisted and turned arbitrarily that almost no consistent usage of the word by all Christians remains.

One of the confusions in the word grace, then, comes from the fact that it has both an adjectival and substantive usage. This confusion is solved by little more than its recognition. While at first sight grace seems to refer to nothing specific in Christian theology because it refers to everything, still, certain clarifications can be made. First of all, one can isolate the simplest and most general meaning of grace; it refers to the fact that God loves human beings and that he deals graciously or lovingly with them. All Christians agree on this: Grace is God's love for us. "The basic sense of Christian grace, whatever its later and further technical or non-scholastic connotations, should always remind us that God first loved us. Let that be its fundamental chord."[2] Grace, then, is God's love for humankind.

This understanding of the word grace is partially responsible for the limitations of this study. It is a historical treatment of grace limited to the period beginning with Augustine and stretching to the present and does not include a study of the New or Old Testament records of the religious experience of grace. Ordinarily one would begin such a study with a scriptural understanding of grace since it is on this data that the history of the theology of grace is dependent. But besides the fact that the inquiry would be too vast for the limits set here, it should be added that the notion of grace as a specific theme in the scriptural period is too undifferentiated for our purposes. And with Augustine, the understanding of grace undergoes a radical shift, one that remained decisive for theology in the West. In the New Testament, grace refers to God's absolutely gratuitous favor in regard to human beings. It describes this quality of God in all of his dealings with humanity in the Christian dispensation. Quite simply, the whole economy in all of its aspects is grace. Cornelius Ernst too has recognized this quality and expresses it well:

> Grace becomes then an open concept capable of embracing the whole of God's gift of himself to man, and so capable of indefinitely various further particularization. It is not as though we were to itemize God's gifts and call one of them "grace"; it is rather that "grace" qualifies the whole of God's self-communication as a gift beyond all telling.[3]

The subject matter of this book, then, is God's love for humanity, but in a very special sense. The book does not look into the areas in which God's love is more or less "objectively" defined in the Christian dispensation, that is, in the central mysteries of Christ, his revelation and his redemption. Rather the history of the theology of grace is really a history of special problems in the Christian experience of how God deals with people concretely in this world. In that history, the word grace is used much more directly as a substantive and denotes the specific ways in which God's love manifests itself in the life of human beings and its effects in humanity and history. In this history, grace tends toward having an objective sense in its own right almost (but never completely) apart from the central mysteries of Christianity. The problematics of the theology of grace can be seen as attempts to define exactly what the relation is between God and persons, and concretely *how* his love manifests itself in ongoing Christian experience. Reductively, the history of the question of grace is really the question of Christian spirituality, that is, the understanding of the nature of human existence in relation to God through Christ and his Spirit—*how* God deals with us lovingly. It asks what exactly is God's love for us and accordingly how should we regard ourselves in this light. From this it can be seen that the study of the theology of grace is really a study in fundamental themes of Christian anthropology, that is, of an understanding of human existence in relation to God in the light of Christian experience.

The subject of this book, then, is the love of God for humanity in a very special sense. It studies specific problems in the Christian experience of God, problems of such a fundamental nature that they help define in their most fundamental sense Christian spirituality and anthropology.

The Experience of Grace

Experience is the basis of all knowledge; experience is the principle of meaning, of understanding and communication. The word "experience" is used here in a very general sense. What is asserted is that in order to say that something is known or that a reality spoken of is grasped or understood, there must be some interior and personal contact with it. Knowledge and learning demand that reality in some way reverberate within the subjectivity of the knower. Inversely, there can be no knowledge without some sort of experience of that which is known. This principle is universal and absolute and can be applied to theological data as well: Unless there is some experience of grace, the phenomenon cannot be understood, communicated or spoken about. If grace is not experienced in any way, the word grace will simply have no meaning. By experience, however, we do not necessarily mean direct or emotional reaction to something. There are many different kinds of experience, and, correspondingly, there are many different kinds of knowledge. The meaning of the word experience, then, is left very general and the principle says simply that any reality spoken about must be interiorly appropriated in some way for words concerning it to make sense.

The first question that arises concerning grace and experience is whether or not grace can be experienced at all. This question is most important because the very nature of the problem entailed has far-ranging implications.

There has been a long and strong tradition that says that grace cannot be experienced. And there are good reasons for asserting this. Scholasticism traditionally held that grace was supernatural and what is supernatural by definition exceeds direct human experience. Thus Fransen can write of the dynamism of grace: "Let us repeat: This dynamism, as such, escapes our immediate and clear consciousness. A first reason is that the dynamic commitment is of a nature that cannot be the object of immediate experience."[4]

There are other reasons for saying that grace cannot be experienced. Because God works within human existence, because God works according to our nature and even according to the contours of our personality, without coercion and often adjusting himself to the inner life of a person, God's action cannot be distinguished from the dynamisms of human nature and personality itself. God's action in a person is that person's action; seen from an anthropological point of view, anyone's "divine" way of acting under the influence of the Spirit, however extraordinary the behavior may seem, is still that person's behavior.[5] Still another reason, closely related to what has already been said, argues that there is nothing against which to oppose and compare the experience of ourselves under grace since grace is universally operative in human existence. This argument is advanced against a conception of human-existence-out-of-grace or in a state of "pure nature" against which existence-in-grace could be compared and grace distinguished. It is meant to break down the sharp distinction or separation between grace and profane history, the "supernatural" and the natural worlds.[6] If this argument is pushed to its logical conclusion, grace would not be experienced at all precisely because there would be nothing to which it would be opposed.

In all of these arguments there is one fundamental point that must always be kept in mind. In no sense is it easy to distinguish grace or the action of God in one's life clearly. There is an element of nonexperience in every experience of grace, a dialectical element of "human nature" or "personality" that obscures grace from our direct view. As a result, every form of religious or quasi-religious experience cannot be simply identified with genuine movements from God. If every personal religious experience is taken as an authentic manifestation of grace, one opens the way to the greatest possible error and disillusionment. Illuminism quickly descends into illusionism. All discernment of authentic religious experience requires extreme caution and the application of both critical and pragmatic norms. All of the reasoning against the possibility of experiencing grace has this value of cautioning against the easy possibility of falling victim to pseudoreligious experience, to fantasy or illusion on the one hand, or to idolatry on the other.

But once this caution has been entered and insisted upon, one must on the contrary insist that the position of the nonexperience of grace is profoundly wrong. For, quite simply, if God's grace, that is, his loving communication with human existence cannot be experienced, then the Christian God cannot be known at all. If God's grace cannot be experienced and somehow known as such, then there is no way of speaking about knowing "the will of God," and the whole process of religious discernment becomes fraudulent psychologism. In short, without an experience of God's grace, human existence is cut off from all communication with the Christian God.

It must be said, then, that grace can be experienced. It can even be experienced and known with surety, if by that is meant that certain qualities and intensity in religious experience can produce an absolute certainty in the matter for any given individual. But at the same time, grace cannot be experienced "immediately" or "directly," and there is always need to apply criteria for judgment. As Rahner says, grace is experienced, but not as grace.[7] The force of this statement lies in its strictly dialectical nature. That is to say, it both affirms and denies the same thing at the same time with the result that one has to enter the realm of religious experience in a spirit of both radical openness and radical critique. While grace cannot be experienced apart from the equipment of the human personality, still, the specificity of the movement of God can be discerned within that experience and is capable of being named. The criteria for this discernment, however, cannot be examined here.[8]

While this solution, which is basically that of Blondel and Rahner, resolves the dilemma of the understanding, it leaves open the more serious problem of discernment in the concrete. All simplification must be avoided here; the theoretical solution does not solve the problem involved in concrete and individual cases of trying to distinguish authentic movements of grace. Can one really know whether this or that in the concrete is the will of God? and not my will? And has one the right to surrender responsibility in decision to a will other than one's own if that cannot be clearly known? How does one decide in this particular movement or experience that it is a manifestation of grace and that it is not escapist, involving a surrender of autonomous and solid rational judgment? A moment's reflection on the questions of religious vocation, of important decisions in life, of the whole movement of religious discernment, will show that the issue of the experience of grace is profoundly important and has the deepest consequences for the spiritual life. The position taken here, without going into concrete detail, is that grace can be experienced and known as such, even while this is very difficult and always subject to the possibility of illusion.

The reason why one must turn to experience in the study of grace is that an understanding of the meaning of the word grace, that is, a grasp of the reality of the love of God touching human life and an understanding of how it occurs, demands that one have some experience of it. And if people want to communicate with others about this reality, either theologically or pastorally, they must be in touch with both their own experience and the experience of those with whom they would communicate, that is, if their words are to have any meaning.

For nonbelievers the word grace and the language of grace ultimately have no meaning; or the meaning is so abstract and distant that it lacks the concrete validity needed to be affirmed as true. It may even be said of many Christians that they hear but do not have any concrete experience or correlated understanding of the meaning of the language of grace. The words of grace as they resound in Scripture and the liturgy, in the creed and in doctrine, may be passively received and assented to, but have little relation whatever to their religious experience. It may be that their own deepest religious experience is tinged with doubt, and what does that have to do with the grace of Christ? An ever-new basis, then, for understanding and communicating what grace means must be sought in an examination of religious experience of people, that is, an examination of the "signals of transcendence," as Berger calls them, so that the real meaning of Christian words and language about grace may be attached to them.

In the area of religious experience, which for our purposes may be identified with the experience of grace, the work of William James is preeminent. He has examined in phenomenological detail the abundant testimony of how grace has been operative in human lives. Indeed, so manifold are the ways in which grace may be experienced that once again the problem is posed of how to determine real or normative or authentic Christian experience from its counterfeits. Apropos of James, then, some more probing into the relation of experience and Christian theology is necessary.

William James and the Experience of Grace

William James's Gifford Lectures on *The Varieties of Religious Experience*[9] make up a volume that is a classic in religious literature. Cast in an informal style and an elegant prose, the work is a pioneer effort in the psychology of religion as well as the philosophy of religion. In the remarks that follow, no attempt will be made to summarize James's work, which deserves to be studied in its own right. Rather, the observations made here are simply meant to highlight certain themes that appear in this work that have a bearing on the study of the theology of grace.

Description of Religious Experience

Undoubtedly the most important element of James's work for our purposes is his lengthy descriptions of the variety of religious experience itself. In the manifold testimony that he has gathered one sees as it were directly how the divine, how the love of God—or, as the Christian would say, grace—operates in human lives in many different ways. It is quite important that one understand why this is the case.

James answers this question of variety and difference when he explains why it is that he as a psychologist and an empirical philosopher may embark upon a study of religious phenomena. Religious feelings and experiences, he says, whatever their quality and whatever else they may be, are still human emotions and experiences. They are not experiences that occur outside of this world.[10] Moreover, in refuting biological and psychological reductionism and establishing the distinction between the origin on the one hand and the value and truth of an experience on the other, James points out that every experience, opinion and even scientific doctrine without exception "flows from the state of its possessor's body at the time . . . . There is not a single one of our states of mind, high or low, healthy or morbid, that has not some organic process as its condition."[11] For this reason religious experience can be described and analyzed like any other human emotion. This does not mean, of course, that psychology or natural science can provide an adequate explanation of religious experience; this is precisely the position that James refutes. As far as a theology of grace is concerned, the point of significance in James's explanation is that there is an experience of grace and it is a human experience, one that occurs in this world. The experience of grace is *human* experience.

This roughly corresponds to the common and traditional axiom of Scholastic theology that grace builds on nature, and what is said of human nature can be applied concretely to human personality. Grace does not supplant personality; it works through it. It should not be implied from this that grace cannot suddenly redirect a whole personality as in conversion, nor that it might not be responsible for sudden new movements within a person's life, movements contrasting greatly with old patterns. But even when this does occur, and whatever the motion of grace, it will have a physiological, psychological and personal basis as well. Even when grace works with seeming force and violence, it will still manifest itself through the agencies or mechanisms of temperament, taste, personality and biography.[12] This has momentous consequences because it is the root and ground of a genuine pluralism in the experience of God and his grace. It should not be surprising to find real variety and even great differences in the experience of the same love of God.

There are two areas, one of a practical and another of a more theoretical nature, where these differences are of import. First of all, practically speaking or on a pastoral level, the variety in religious experience means that one should be slow to prejudge on the basis of a priori principles where the Spirit of God may be moving another. There is a uniqueness in everyone's experience of God's love and it is to the credit of Ignatius in his *Spiritual Exercises* that he recognized this.

A second implication of a more theoretical nature applies to theology. If theology is to be closely related to experience, and if experience is pluralistic, then pluralism must be written into even the Christian theology or understanding of grace, that is, of how God's love operates in the world. Again, this does not mean that there is no common element in Christian experience or that no parameters or definitions of limits can be assigned. But it does seem to mean that these norms of orthodoxy must be general enough to include a variety of different experiences and understandings; they certainly cannot define a uniformity in the operation of God's love. As God's love is experienced in a manifold of different ways, so too will its operations be understood.

That this is a real problem is seen when one tries to seek, theologically, normative understandings of Christian experience, or to understand how definite doctrine can be announced. For example, the theology of liberation, which is closely connected with the experience of grace, tries to establish as normative that the Christian experience involves the Christian in the world and its developmental and political processes. But what if most Christians experience grace only on Sunday and in sacramental practices, that is, in a realm cut off from human involvement on any social level? This is, of course, the definition of a problem and not a suggestion of a solution. That is to say, given a situation of pluralism, theology cannot be totally satisfied with it, but must seek after the normative within it. As to the specific problem mentioned here, we shall return to it in the concluding chapter.

A final comment on James's descriptions of religious experience concerns his psychological analyses and categorizations of types. It should be recalled that in James's time psychology was an infant science and he, one of its pioneers. These lectures were written about the same time that Freud was putting the finishing touches on *The Interpretation of Dreams*. An indication of his genius is that James was working with psychological tools and categories that were scarcely developed as they are today. One should, therefore, take congnizance of the categories and the method that he is using. For example, when James describes contrasting types of religious experience, these are merely "types," that is to say, abstract classifications based on descriptions that help in speaking about differences of experience. They should not, however, be reified—in actuality experience is too complex and interwoven with many elements. Thus when James contrasts Protestant and Catholic types of religious experience, we must be aware that, while these generalizations may be helpful indicators of differences, they are not definitions, and real and clearer differences will be better seen in the realm of theology. We shall treat these differences in chapter 4.

Doctrinal Elements in Experience

In reading James's descriptions of religious experience, one finds in them many of the basic themes of the history of Christian theology and doctrine. It might be useful to point out some of these themes.

The fundamental Christian doctrine of grace is that God's love for humanity is absolutely gratuitous, that is, it is unmerited and unclaimed by any right on the part of a person and unexacted or freely given on the part of God. The classical doctrine is one of "double gratuity," that is, not only did God freely create man; over and above that, he bestows on humanity his love anew or in a special way through the Christian dispensation. This theme of gratuity occurs again and again in James's descriptions of religious experience, so much so that he takes it to be a constant or stable psychological characteristic of religious experience—it is like a new *gift* added to life.[13] Contact with God, being a gift, is beyond one's control; it is spontaneous, coming and going as a spirit that blows where it will. In explaining this quality, James constantly reverts to the analogy of love itself, which always comes as a surprise.[14]

Another doctrine concerning grace is that it is healing. In terms of the doctrine of the Fall and human propensity to sin, grace comes as a healing and sanative power enabling freedom to open up toward the good, to open up beyond selfishness toward Love. It is not difficult to see this doctrine in the phenomenology and analysis of the sick soul, the divided self, and the process of conversion. In fact, Paul and Augustine, who are the originators of this doctrine as we have it, are in a sense the classical examples of an experience that, of course, extends far beyond their persons. Here again James finds an almost universally common element in religious experience.[15]

A third theme in the theology of grace, especially in Catholic doctrine, is that grace is elevating. As will be seen, the Scholastic understanding of this is in abstract metaphysico-ontological terms that can scarcely be experienced. But this system of understanding cannot be separated from the more concrete terms like a "New Creation," the "New Man" and the "New Life" of grace that are found in the New Testament. In the testimonies of mystical experience, which is religious experience raised to a higher degree, this theme of a new life and being raised up by communion with the God who fills one's being with himself is again a permanent element.[16]

In pointing out these doctrinal themes in religious experience, it is not our intention to reduce the meaning of these doctrines to such experiences alone. Christian theology is not Christian if it is simply a phenomenology of religious experience, and is not theology if it does not apply other criteria for understanding and judging. But viewed the other way around, if Christian doctrine says that God's grace is universally operative in the lives of people, and that it is a gratuitously offered love that is healing and elevating, surely these qualities will appear somewhere. And one can say with certainty that they appear in Christian doctrine because they were first experienced in Christian lives.

The Relation of Experience and Theology

This is not the place to develop a theory of the relation between experience and theology, and ordinarily a philospher of religion would not be a final authority for such a theory. James does not offer the best theory of religious experience and one can find better philosophical or theological understandings of religious experience in such authors as Augustine, Schleiermacher, Tillich or Rahner. But the question is raised by James. Since this discussion will presently shift to Augustine and the domain of theology, and since practically everything James says is more or less presupposed by many theologians today, certain elements of this relation should at least be underlined without going further into this vast topic.

First of all, just as he is critical of scientism—the reduction of reality to what can be known by science—so too is James critical of rationalism—the idea that the only criterion of what can be known is reason. The horizon of reality cannot be limited to what rational thought can clearly set before our minds. Reason alone cannot uncover all there is to know.[17] In the same vein, it will be noticed that "theology" and "dogmatics" are pejorative words for James. This is so because they represent as far as he is concerned a method of theology that proceeds from abstract principles or objective formulae, that is, devoid of concrete experience or subjective life, and that deductively arrives at conclusions that are equally unrelated to human life and have no significance for it. For James the theologian is one who prejudges experience and reality on the basis of a priori principles.[18] This criticism will not appear new; it is rather standard today. As a matter of fact, James says that, as far as religious argument is concerned, no one can be convinced of God's reality by arguments of pure reason. Reason and intellect merely formulate and rationalize what one believes already. "The unreasoned and immediate assurance is the deep thing in us, the reasoned argument is but a surface exhibition."[19] Much the same conclusions were established by Cardinal Newman in his *Grammar of Assent* when he analyzed informal inference.

Experience, then, goes before system of thought. And the basis of religious philosophies or theologies will be found in an underlying, and in that sense prior, concrete experience. It may be that James's ideas of experience here is a bit narrow, for certainly "mind" and "intellect" introduce us into levels of meaning and value that are real and that cannot be perceived or experienced without them. But at the same time, all processes of reasoning, and theological formulae for that matter, must relate somehow to concrete life experience.

For James religious experience is personal, ineffable, more or less incommunicable, and therefore authoritative only for the person who has the experience. This is seen in his very definition of religion and his treatment of mysticism.[20] This experience is the basis of religion, its deeper source, and "philosophic and theological formulas are secondary products, like translations of a text into another tongue."[21] The function of theological discourse is to render experience and its object public, communicable, objective, universally acceptable and applicable. While such reasoned discourse is secondary, still it is a necessary part of religion since one must speak, communicate and use general or abstract language. But since theological discourse is secondary and as it were after the fact of experience, it is of its nature grounded in experience and must be related to it for its meaning and validity.[22] Systems of theology appear as "hypotheses" or "over-beliefs" that try to comprehend and explain religious experience and its object coherently, that is, in sympathy with other data that one knows about the world. Theology and doctrine then are expressions of actual religious experience in a more or less adequate way. And just as no philosophy's reason is entirely objective or universally accepted, so, too, one can expect pluralism in religion, theology and doctrine.[23]

By and large this is an acceptable view of the relation between theology and experience. One may argue with or wish further refinement of the idea of hypothesis, but, in all, the structure of the relationship that James outlines corresponds to much of contemporary theological thinking. A more serious question is whether James has not viewed religion and religious experience too individualistically. In response to this question it might be recalled, first of all, that James's definition of religion as experience "in solitude" is a conscious option in view of the definite goal of undermining the claims of scientism and rationalism.[24] Second, he admits that religion is also a public and social and institutional phenomenon and simply does not choose to treat of those aspects. And, third, much of what is labeled pejoratively "individualistic" in James might be cast in a better light if it were viewed as "personalistic." James rightly places the locus of religious experience in the person, for it cannot occur anywhere else. A common social consciousness can be viewed as distinct from persons, but it cannot exist apart from individual persons.

But after this is said, the deliberate exclusion of religion as a social phenomenon is still a lacuna in James's work. This limitation closes off the consideration of community experience and of the relation between personal and communal experience, which is important for the individual and has much to do with theological judgments. Occasionally, too, a real individualism shows itself in James's thought, as for example when he says, "Our responsible concern is with our private destiny, after all."[25] Such a sentiment is profoundly unchristian, almost antichristian. And yet this is somehow offset by his description of saintliness, in which lies the value of religion, in terms of a service to society and the future of the world.

The Empirical Cast of Mind

In one sense William James's empirical cast of mind is an Anglo-Saxon trait and James relates his philosophy to the British Empiricist tradition.[26] But at the same time, this tendency to return to concrete experience corresponds well with the Catholic movement away from its past abstract and objective theological expression as found in Scholasticism and its demand for reform of theology in the light of the concrete experience of people in the contemporary world. What is needed is a theology that relates to the lives of people today, to their experience of the world that is real and actual. In this context, James says: "So long as we deal with the cosmic and the general, we deal only with the symbols of reality, but as soon as we deal with private and personal phenomena as such, we deal with realities in the completest sense of the term."[27]

In recommending an empirical cast of mind, we are using the term "empirical" in a somewhat looser and wider sense than is ordinarily the case. Usually the empirical is that which can be perceived by the senses. Here we mean an attitude of mind that turns to the concrete and actual world as one criterion for understanding, but not in the sense that one should limit experience in this world to what is available to sense experience alone. There are areas in which James's empiricism seems to be a hindrance to theological understanding, as, for example, in his theory of grace working in the subconscious. While structurally his understanding is very suggestive and contains valuable elements, still, the way he expresses himself seems coarse and primitive, seeming as it does to lean on a physical or physiological analogy. While grace undoubtedly works with human personality, more refinement is required than James provides in order to understand this.

On the whole, however, James's turn to actual experience is of great value for generating new perspectives in theological understanding. An example of this is offered in the concrete and existentialist quality of James's understanding of religion. This is seen most clearly in his treatment of prayer. Prayer for James is any kind of actual communion or conversation or interchange with God. This actual dialogue with God is the essence of religion; it *is* religion. It is its actuality because it is religion in act. Where it is lacking, there is no religion.[28] Translated into Christian terms, one could say that Christianity is the Christian life, there where grace becomes real and actual.

What James says on prayer is closely connected with his views on saintliness and pragmatism. Here, I believe, one has arrived at the heart of James's thought, as it appears in this work at least, and here the value of his empirical cast of mind comes to the fore.

In his chapter on conversion, James asks whether or not a sudden conversion is a work of divine intrusion into human personality, whether or not it is a miracle of grace.[29] Is such a conversion an actual "sanctification?"[30] His answer is clear. It is not the suddenness or slowness that makes conversion real. The ultimate test of religious value is not how it happens but its fruits, that is, what is attained. If a person is really born anew, this will become manifest in his life.[31] It is in the saint that one has, as it were, a concrete and actual manifestation of grace, and it is grace for the world. The saints are the authors and increasers of goodness in this world. They mediate goodness. Empirically, they are a genuine creative force for society; they tend to make real and actual a degree of virtue, an ideal and a quality of goodness that would not be assumed as even possible without them. "They are the impregnators of the world, vivfiers and animators of potentialities of goodness which but for them would lie forever dormant."[32] The saint is "an effective ferment of goodness, a slow transmuter of the earthly into a more heavenly order . . . . One fire kindles another; and without that overtrust in human worth which they show, the rest of us would lie in spiritual stagnancy."[33]

In James's description of the value of saintliness, which for him signifies as well the meaning and the truth of religion, one can see what the empirical cast of mind consists in and where it leads. It asks what is true in terms of what is real, what is actual and what can be experienced. In large measure this is what a critical theology also demands, and this is what is demanded of it.

With this general understanding of the "experience of grace" we now turn to a discussion of the problem of grace and how we might come to understand the "language of grace."

The Problem of Grace

In order to learn anything, and in order to understand it, there must be a question in the learner or some consciousness of a problem. While this is presented here as a principle of learning, it can also be justified as a principle of knowledge, for understanding always involves fiting data into some pattern, heuristic structure or unifying "theory." Put more simply, it can be said that in order to understand the solution to a problem (and all data are problems for the understanding) or the answer to a question, one must first have an appreciation of the problem itself. The question or, better, active questioning is the very supposition of all learning and without it there will be little more than the receiving of words, perhaps the memorization of formulae, that have little or no meaning. It is commonplace to say that the most important thing in theology is not to know the solutions but to have a grasp of the problems. This is true and has to be taken seriously.

The deepest and most fundamental problem of grace itself is the problem of the goodness of God. The question is: Is God good? and How does one know that God is good? Doctrinally and to the extent that one remains a Christian of faith, it is hard to see how a person could hold anything else. But still it should be realized that these questions correspond to real existential problems that often exist inside or within a core of faith. The problem is real precisely because of the concrete and actual experience of evil in the world. The problem of evil is and always has been an embarrassment to religion. And the question that evil raises will never be appreciated unless it is seen as radically challenging the problem of goodness and the goodness of God.

Concretely, if one tries to speak of the goodness of God to the poor and to those conscious of being oppressed, to the crippled, to the utterly deprived, to those who have suffered some deep tragedy, or are on the border of despair because all meaning has gone out of life, he or she may find that the goodness of God is problematic; it is a problem. Without being rhetorical about this, it must be said that one should not be too cavalier in the way one pronounces that God is good and deals with humanity lovingly. Moreover, even when we sincerely believe and can assert God's goodness with confidence, we should have some ability to explain *how* God is good and *how* this can be experienced and known. For those who do not experience that grace and that love will probably say, "Show me," and to the extent that one cannot, the words lose much if not all of their meaning. Evil, suffering, sin and death are *realities*; they are the causes of doubt to faith and the reasons of atheism; and they are solid reasons constituting the challenge to any doctrine of grace. And these realities are experienced and felt by all, even those inside the realm of faith and consequently inside the Church. A doctrine of grace must be one that is founded on equally experienced realities.

The special problems of grace are the problems that are met in the course of studying the history of its theology. They are such problems as that of God's action within human beings over against our own freedom and autonomy. Does God toy with persons as with a puppet on the end of a string? What is the relation between the so-called supernaturality of the Christian economy and the natural world? These questions and the others that will be studied are fundamental, structural and perduring questions. This means that even though they are studied in particular past historical contexts, still, the answers to these questions involve basic definitions of understandings of human existence and our relationship to God. They are perennial; they are never completely solved.

The Language of Grace

Closely connected with the special problems of grace is the question of the language of grace. Each of the problems we shall consider arose in history and received its more or less traditional responses in very definite and limited contexts. When notions and basic ideas were worked out in past historical contexts, the restrictions and limitations of those contexts of understanding were at the same time written into the Christian language of grace. As a matter of fact, the concept of grace has been so narrowly defined that often the historical meaning and usage of the language of grace does not at all illuminate the reality we experience today but only serves to obscure it. Quite simply, then, much of the traditional language of grace is out of date and in some cases it is unintelligible to an intelligent contemporary person. Thus a main problem in this book on the theology of grace is simply that of coming to terms with the meaning of the language of the tradition of the Church on grace as it was defined along the way which the problems that arose in different epochs charted for it.

It should be noted that the word "language" is used here to mean more than word symbols construed in systems for communication, that is, language in the ordinary sense. The word is used metaphorically to include beyond ordinary language both cultural and theological understanding. The whole system of meaning, from both culture and theology, that is involved in a historical context is included in the logic of what is here called language.

History

Our task in investigating the Christian theology of grace is most fundamentally historical. The Christian language and theology of grace come from the past; at any given time, contemporary language is always determined by the past and to understand it one must understand its genesis. "Tradition," then, is a healthy term referring as it does to the basic datum of a continuity in historical Christian life and understanding, and to the fact that there is something common and normative in the past from which we have to learn. An introduction to the theology of grace assumes the responsibility of entering into the past theologies of grace whose legacies determine present conceptions of the fundamental realities of Christian life and spirituality.

The entry into the past is no easy task because the historical conditions and the languages they generated are no longer ours, nor are the problems, however universal, conceived in exactly the same terms. Given the difficulty of the task of history itself, it would be impossible to cover the whole of the history of the theology of grace.

We have chosen certain peak moments in this history in which the great theologians of the West have formulated understandings that subsequently determined in large measure the history that followed them, even up to the present.

To say that our task is historical also means that it is not systematic. Our aim is *not* to develop a unified and coherent doctrine of grace. Whether or not that is even possible in any comprehensive way is questionable. What will be seen is that there are many possible languages of grace, or systems for understanding the relation between us and God. Simply to illustrate this point, here are some of the many fundamentally different models that people have used to understand this relationship:

—*A metaphorical understanding*: proposed, for example, by Jesus in his parables. God is our Father; we, his children.

—*A metaphysico-ontological understanding*: found in Aquinas and the Scholastics. The relationship between God and human nature is defined in terms of being. God's grace becomes a new elevating ontological nature.

—*Understanding in terms of special problems*: found, for example, in Augustine. Augustine viewed grace in the context of human freedom and its ability to gain salvation. God's grace becomes healing and liberating.

—*An understanding in terms of justice*: Anselm, for example, conceives of our relationship to God because of what Christ has done for us almost in a legal way, or at least in terms of the requirements of feudal justice, right and obligation.

—*An interpersonal framework*: as, for example, in Luther, where God relates to human beings by addressing to them his Word of forgiveness. God is mercy and we the forgiven, and his forgiveness is liberating.

—*An economic understanding*: according to Marx God becomes the tool of the wealthy ruling class to help control the masses and establish law, order and stability.

—*A psychological understanding*: the relationship is one of projection between us and God. For Feuerbach it is a matter of social psychology, for God is the projection of the race, an ideal form of "humanity." For Freud, God is the projection of the father image that one needs and on which one is dependent.

The point is that there are any number of languages in which to understand grace. All of the conceptions seen above contain some truth; all of them highlight some aspect of the Christian relationship to God that others do not. All of those aspects that are highlighted precisely because they spring out of different systems of understanding cannot be brought into one system of understanding. But history can try to enter each one and try to understand it on its own terms. More and more, Burke says, because of historical consciousness, grace is being understood as a whole economy of God dealing with humanity as it moves along in history. Particular historical appreciations of what grace is—that is, how God deals with us—will come and go, will be fashioned for each period. "Grace, then, rather comprises the whole history of God's dealing with man."[34]

Because of the difficulty of understanding the past, and because of the vastness of history of the theology of grace, this book will focus on only four theologians. These theologians are chosen because of their stature on the presumption that in entering the world of these great thinkers one touches on the substance of the history of a given period and on all the central issues of a given topic.

Theology

This book in not only historical, it is also theological. Theology may be defined as the attempt to understand faith: *Fides quaerens intellectum*. In this case, theology is an attempt to understand what has been called grace, that is, how it is that God deals lovingly with human beings, and how they are to be understood in relation to the Christian God. To understand what another person wrote in the past is to gain historical knowledge. To understand the matter itself about which he spoke, for oneself, is quite another thing. Theology involves making judgments about what is true.

It will be noticed as this book unfolds that history is quite arbitrary and accidental, determined as it is by external circumstances and the wills of concrete persons. History is pluralistic. While the Christian may assume that there is a basically self-identical principle (the Spirit of Christ) and a continuous Christian experience of it across history, still, this expresses itself in very different ways throughout history. The unity of Christian experience across history is not at all evident. Theology, then, is critical understanding; it does not simply accept past statements; it interprets them and passes judgment upon them. Theology, to be theology and not merely history, cannot be simply a review of the meaning of the word grace from the Old Testament to the present, for because a certain meaning of grace appears in some past document, this does not imply for theology that that meaning is relevant for our way of looking at the world today. And this is so whether that document be the Old Testament, the New Testament or from the history of dogma.

Theology, then, is critical; that is to say, it questions the meaning of past expression. And in every case the main criterion (although not the only criterion) for such a questioning and subsequent judgment of relevance is whether or not it corresponds with contemporary experience of the matter and with the data and facts that make up our world. Because of the gap that separates the past from our present self-understanding, theology constantly asks the question of whether or not past understandings are valid for us today as they appear or whether they must be demythologized, interpreted in new and different contexts, reduced to more general understandings, or put aside as mistaken or merely curious. This critical understanding must begin with our own contemporary experience. Thus Gilkey, in assessing our contemporary situation, has written:

> Our theological analysis must begin with man. If we felt sure that the divine word in Scripture was the truth, then the Bible might be our starting point. Or if we felt some assurance that existence as a whole was coherent, a metaphysical beginning might be possible. But in our situation, these two certainties are lacking. What remains for us, as remained for Augustine and Schleiermacher in not unsimilar straits, is man as we can see him acting out his life around him, and as we feel the shape and depth of that human existence in ourselves.[35]

In our last chapter we shall try to begin a reconstructive effort at an understanding of grace in the context of history.

The Object of This Book

To conclude this introductory chapter, some of the objectives that these historical essays are intended to serve may be enumerated.

To a large extent they are the aims of any essay into history. And because they are existential, they will only be mediated through the active dialogue of the reader with these thinkers of the past.

This book is to a large extent simply a reflection on religious experience and this is considered a value and end in itself. The gain from such an exercise is personal and existential and may not even be able to be objectified into a permanent content that will be carried away from the reading. If such reflection does result in solid understanding, so much the better.

Second, an objective of this essay is to initiate one into a reading of and dialogue with the great theologians of the past. The book is geared to stimulate a kind of "seeing" and "experiencing" and "understanding" of the phenomenon of God's dealing with human beings through the minds of the most influential thinkers of Western Christianity, the people who have determined for us and for most Christians up to the present time our understanding of what is called grace. Again, this result will be experiential, an experience; its lasting result will not be had in retaining in one's mind the historical content contained in these writings. That will be quickly forgotten.

Third, perhaps the most important objective of this book is to negotiate or mediate an experience of the diversity and pluralism of historical understanding, and this within a single Christian tradition. The purpose is to illustrate this, to demonstrate it, for this is something that must be experienced; one cannot be told about it. A careful study of history can only show that Christian self-understanding twists and turns with history itself so that the continuity of Christianity's understanding of itself must be sought after; it is not obvious.

Fourth, another experience that flows from the experience of historical consciousness is one of liberation. The study of history is liberating because in the recognition of the arbitrary and accidental quality of past expression, the degree to which it is determined by historical circumstances, and the degree to which it is alien from the present precisely because of this, one realizes to the very same extent that the past is past and one is not bound by it. The study of history liberates from history to the extent that one grasps that every past expression is bound to a particular set of determining circumstances that no longer prevail, and to the extent that one sees the vast differences in understanding that are introduced in every era according to its particular and peculiar situation. In short, we do not study past languages in order to be bound by their literal form, nor their particular syntax and usage. Rather we study to learn the experience beneath them, that is, their depth meaning, and then to be freed from them.

A fifth objective of this book is also very general and at the same time experiential; that is, it is mediated by indirection. It is designed to demonstrate indirectly the nature of theology. Theology as a discipline is complicated; it has many functions. But theology as a task is quite simple; it is an attempt to understand Christian faith and reality in the light of it. Its tools are faith experience, history and critical reason. On the basis of our contemporary experience, we look at historical expressions of the faith and try to make critical judgments about what can be said today in their light. It is a rational attempt, in faith, to find from what is true, beneath the varied expressions of the past, that which can be asserted as corresponding to our experience of the world today.

Along this line, a sixth objective of this book is to gather along the way those themes in the theology of grace that remain more or less constant through history. A good indication that something is essential in Christian experience is the pragmatic test of time; if something perdures through the varying circumstances of history, it is probably something that belongs to the substance of the Christian experience of grace. One of the objectives of this book, then, will be to try to grasp and synthesize the major and common themes in the various theologies of grace.

And, finally, an aim of this book is to communicate some objective content. One learns from history; in fact, one has no other source from which to learn except sheer immediacy. All formed knowledge is constituted by the past and this past may tell us what our contemporary experience should be. An existential dialectic may be seen operative in one's study of the past. On the one hand, detailed historical knowledge quickly slips from the memory. On the other hand, while the objective content of history may soon be forgotten, many basic experiences mediated through that history should remain. It is for this reason that the preceding objectives are by far the more important.

With these objectives in mind, then, we pass now to Augustine of Hippo and how he experienced and spoke about the phenomenon of grace.

Notes

1. Peter Fransen, *The New Life of Grace* (Tournai: Desclee & Company, 1969), p. 15.

2. Ibid.

3. Cornelius Ernst, *The Theology of Grace* (Notre Dame, Ind.: Fides Publishers, Inc., 1974), p. 29.

4. Fransen, *New Life of Grace*, p. 248. It should be noted that Fransen's statement contains several qualifications.

5. Ibid.

6. "So in our experience there does not exist any term of comparison that would enable us to know what concrete transformation in us is due to God's grace" (Juan Luis Segundo, *Grace and the Human Condition* [Maryknoll, N.Y.: Orbis Books, 1973], p. 14).

7. Karl Rahner, "Concerning the Relationship between Nature and Grace," *Theological Investigations* I (Baltimore: Helicon Press, 1961), p. 300.

8. Ignatius of Loyola's rules for the discernment of spirits as well as his methods for making a basic decision or election can be considered as methods of knowing authentic movements of grace. And Rahner's "The Logic of Concrete Individual Knowledge in Ignatius Loyola" is a carefully worked out theological explanation of how grace can be experienced and known within that framework. See Karl Rahner, *The Dynamic Element in the Church* (New York: Herder and Herder, 1964), pp. 84–170.

9. William James, *The Varieties of Religious Experience* (New York: Collier Books, 1961).

10. Ibid., pp. 37–38.

11. Ibid., p. 30

12. See ibid., pp. 357–358.

13. Ibid., p. 377.

14. See ibid., pp. 330–331.

15. Ibid., p. 393.

16. See ibid., pp. 393–394.

17. See ibid., pp. 73–77.

18. See ibid., chap. 18, passim.

19. Ibid., pp. 75, 341–343.

20. See ibid., chaps. 16 and 17; also, p. 42.

21. Ibid., p. 337.

22. Ibid., pp. 338–339.
23. Ibid., pp. 341, 378–381.
24. Ibid., pp. 381–389, esp. p. 389.
25. Ibid., p. 388.
26. Ibid., pp. 346–347.
27. Ibid., p. 386.
28. Ibid., p. 361.
29. Ibid., p. 189.
30. Ibid., p. 198.
31. Ibid., pp. 197–198.
32. Ibid., p. 284.
33. Ibid., pp. 284–285.
34. E. M. Burke, "Grace," *The New Catholic Encyclopedia*, vol. 6 (New York: McGraw-Hill Book Co., 1967), p. 658b.
35. Langdon Gilkey, "Dissolution and Reconstruction in Theology," *Christian Century 82*(Feb. 3, 1965): 137.

2

Augustine: Grace and Human Autonomy

When people open Augustine, they are faced on almost any given page with some of the deepest questions about the nature of human existence, of God and of our relationship with him. Because of Augustine's questioning and probing character, most of the conclusions he reached have a certain timeless quality about them. And on the question of grace, his thoughts were written into the doctrine of Western Christianity. Because of the experiential quality of his thought, so attached as it is to his own life experience, his theology has a kind of perennial contemporaneity and vital relatedness that has made him probably the most influential theologian since Paul.

This is particularly true of the question of grace as it is presented in the Pelagian controversy. In one sense, this debate can be viewed very narrowly as involving the question of whether or not God's internal grace is prior to and supportive of the exercise of human freedom in faith and the doing of the good. Seen in this way, the councils of Carthage and Orange testify that this problem has been solved; Pelagius lost and he is a heretic. But the question is really much larger. At stake is a much more basic conception of what the very nature of human existence is according to Christianity. Set in the context of human freedom, the Pelagian controversy asked the perennially radical question of the quality of human behavior, and the sources of good and evil in this world. There is no Christian piety or spirituality, nor can one even give a retreat or preach a sermon without explicitly or implicitly working on assumptions that underlie the Pelagian controversy.

Because of the extensiveness of the broader question and because of its implications it must be said that the Pelagian question is not solved. A priori and on the supposition that both Augustine and Pelagius were Christians (Pelagius being the more traditional in more than one respect), and that every heresy is based on some truth, one has to allow Pelagius his say before becoming an Augustinian. And a posteriori, after the issues are sifted, it will appear that the values that both Augustine and Pelagius fought for must really be held in constant tension. It is at this level, then, that the following interpretation of the Pelagian controversy is set. The controversy can be seen as involving two elements or poles that must always be held in tension. The fundamental relationship between these two poles was defined through the Pelagian controversy, but the delicate balance between them is a constant issue and one that has particular relevance for today since, more and more, human existence is being defined as freedom and we are called upon to exercise our autonomy.

The Background

When Augustine and Pelagius arrived in Rome in the 380s they had much in common. Both were provincials, Augustine from Thagaste in Northern Africa, Pelagius from Britain. Pelagius like Augustine could well have come in search of a civil career in the heart of the empire. Both, however, turned out to be religious leaders exercising an enormous spiritual force.

More than anything else they shared a common historical period. Paradoxically, while the Church in the late fourth century was rapidly shifting from the persecuted minority religion that it had been to the state religion of the masses, the tradition of a radical conversion to an authentic Christian life of dedication and perfection was still strong, and Augustine converted to it. The tension of a radical break with the past can be seen in Book VIII of the *Confessions*. Pelagius would be the apostle of the need for just such a conversion.

Time is the fashioner of change and this is particularly so in the case of Augustine. From the new convert, a contemplative as much Plotinian as Christian, to the priest and then the bishop, Augustine faced several turning points in his life and was far different when Rome was sacked in the year 410 from the person he was during the winter of 386–387, and far more different still from the reformer Pelagius. Augustine had always been deeply concerned with the problem of evil in human existence, even from his Manichaean days, and the question of the nature of humanity, in the terms of moral good and evil as he viewed it, formed the context of much of his introspection and his theology. A major shift in his thinking occurred around the years 396–397 while he was intensely engaged in the study of Paul and had occasion to respond to some questions put to him by Simplicianus. For the first time the theme of a total dependency on God is announced with the simplicity and strength of conviction that only a kind of religious experience and personal insight can give. He later testified to the extent that he was influenced by Paul's statement "What do you have that you did not receive? And if you received it, why do you boast as if it were not a gift?" (1 Cor. 4:7).

The mechanics of grace and election were seen by Augustine in terms of the phenomenon of delight. We are commanded to live righteously, but this cannot be achieved without faith. We are commanded to believe,

But who can believe unless he is reached by some calling, by some testimony borne to the truth? Who has it in his power to have such a motive present to his mind that his will shall be influenced to believe? Who can welcome in his mind something which does not give him delight? But who has it in his power to ensure that something that will delight him will turn up, or that he will take delight in what turns up? If those things delight us which serve our advancement towards God, that is due not to our own whim or industry or meritorious works, but to the inspiration of God and to the grace which he bestows. He freely bestows upon us voluntary assent, earnest effort, and the power to perform works of fervent charity.[1]

Of this turning point, TeSelle writes:

All that he had worked out concerning the freedom and bondage of the will, the call of grace and its reception through faith and the infusion of love, came to be seen in a new light; it was not so much modified as brought to what seemed to be a fitting conclusion in the conviction that the will is so bound by custom that it cannot free itself, cannot even receive the promises of grace and seek divine aid, but must be called forth by a divine invitation that is suited to the particular situation of each man, that is issued, therefore, by a providence which has watched over the details of his life from the beginning.[2]

With this conviction and in this light Augustine began to review minutely the whole of his life in terms of grace. His whole life and every moment in it was seen as guided by the providence and grace of God. His understanding of human movement toward Truth and the Good, of conversion, of the Christian life and of our ability to lead it was summed up in the keynote statement "Command what you wish, but give what you command."[3]

Pelagius could only have been disappointed when he caught the drift of that statement.[4] For Pelagius had become a spiritual director and something of a leader in a reform movement. Closely associated with the aristocratic class, he preached against the pagan morality that had infiltrated into the Church with conversions of convenience, a life of authentic Christianity, of Christian perfection, one that appealed to the first families who wanted to stand out above the crowd. While Augustine had retired to a corner of the empire and was immersed in theological reflection, Pelagius was in the capital, in the thick of a degenerating church life, immersed in pastoral activity and spiritual exhortation. He preached the decision that radical conversion demanded; he preached a Christian ideal that stood out against the background of Rome's pagan past; Christianity was a *new* life. It was not surprising that the ideas of the reform movement would be popular among the missionary bishops in southern Italy where Christianity could not but be held out to the unbeliever as a totally new way of life. Nor was it surprising that when the reform movement reached Africa with the refugees from Rome it met a different interpretation of Christian existence, of sin and of grace. For that was a more established church, tired with its long struggle with the Donatists, and it was dominated by the ideas of Augustine.

The Teaching

The Pelagians did not deny grace; they affirmed it. But grace was first of all our own human freedom, our God-given ability to decide between good and evil. For Augustine, while free choice remained, the desire and affections of human beings were locked in a web of sin. The custom and habit of personal sin imprisoned free choice within the narrow confines of sensible self-seeking. For the Pelagians, religion and Christianity were mainly an affair of adults, and meant conversion to and baptism into a radically *new* life. The Christian should steadily advance in perfection through self-discipline and asceticism. Augustine, who had once shared elements of this idealism, was now convinced that no real perfection was possible in this life. The Pelagians held that Original Sin did not involve personal guilt leading to damnation; human freedom was part of our nature and it remained intact. Infant baptism tended to be regarded as an initiation into the kingdom of God, and the effects of Original Sin as mediated by society. Only adult baptism included the remission of sin. Augustine denied this traditional view: Human nature is fundamentally disordered because of inherited sin and this involves personal guilt so that an unbaptized infant cannot be saved.[5] Human nature suffered from a *gravitas* or weight that pulled it downward even though the spirit is naturally ordained to ascend to the One, the True and the Good. The Pelagians saw the grace of God in his law; more specifically, in the Christian dispensation, people had the grace of Christ's teaching and his example. This external grace appealed to human freedom and a person could follow if he or she wanted to follow. The external bonds of sin, both of one's personal past and those of the wider milieu, could be broken if the Christian had the courage to follow. For Augustine, grace had to be primarily an internal force, for sin held one prisoner from within; a person's will was a prison to itself. This is the center of Augustine's view of grace and the most precise point at which he was at odds with Pelagius. Grace for Augustine was delight in the good, a new form of liberty that required an internal modification of the human will. No one prior to Augustine had really asserted anything quite like this need for an inner working of God within freedom. Although Christ's teaching was certainly an external and public grace as well, still only those who were called and given the very inner force to respond (and these were relatively few) could be saved. Who would be saved and why? This was ultimately hidden in the mysterious counsels of God. "These things, no doubt, happen through the secret providence of God, whose judgments are unsearchable, and His ways past finding out."[6]

The Values

Stating the doctrines of Augustinianism and Pelagianism is dangerous, for it detaches clear and distinct positions from the experience and life-view of those who held them. Each of these opposing doctrines really represents an aspect of a holistic response to the world from within Christian faith. One way to get below the doctrines is to look for the values that are contained within them and on which they are based.

A central value underlying Pelagius's position is a person's freedom, the power of self-determination, in short, human autonomy. For Pelagius, the adult Christian should become a "son of God," that is, an emancipated heir who is now responsible, in the language of the Roman family.[7] As a spiritual director he could not very well exhort other Christians without a sense that he was appealing to other "centers of freedom." In Pelagius's view, to be a Christian must "make a difference" and his conception of conversion and adult baptism fitted with the deep and long Christian tradition of a complete break with the past. Here Pelagius is strikingly contemporary since more and more today human existence is being defined as freedom, an autonomous possibility for self-determination, self-creation and world-fashioning. We can and do control whole areas of our existence and this is not only a personal experience, it is also a human ideal—to create and define oneself. Any solution to the Pelagian question must incorporate into itself this Pelagian value.

By contrast, a central value underlying Augustine's doctrine is his experience of the absoluteness of God and the correlative total dependency of human being on Him. A dominating image used to describe the human relation to God is that of the child or the infant at its mother's breast. While he had been an enthusiastic convert, Augustine came to realize that the ideals of perfection that the mind could conceive and that Christianity promised were eschatological; they would never be realized in this world. Augustine himself had been too tossed about by passion, concupiscence and external circumstances to hope for too much. And as he looked around him he saw that Christians were scarcely different from other people. Augustine stands forth as a realist in the face of Pelagian idealism.

A second value underlying Pelagius's teaching is a concern for the universal possibility of salvation. Here Pelagius's outlook was much wider and more global than that of Augustine; he could not accept a *massa damnata*. And common sense taught him that eternal damnation for unbaptized infants was an affront not only to human beings but also to God. Christianity taught that God's salvific will was universal and its vehicle was seen by Pelagius in human nature itself, which is provided with the gift of freedom. Sin is certainly abroad, but it affects people mainly through the external mechanisms of social influences that leave the internal nature and freedom of a person intact in its core. This being the case, a person could at any given time respond to God's appeal. God, then, is no respecter of persons, choosing some and not others; God appeals to all people of all time in like measure.

By contrast, Augustine came to realize that God's grace is absolutely gratuitous and this was translated into a doctrine of election and predestination. The evidence was on his side, he thought: One had only to look inside oneself and see that sin gripped human existence interiorly and from within. If persons were opened up to the Good, to what is higher and spiritual, this came as a sudden and spontaneous movement over which they had no control. Among the effects of Original Sin was our de facto disordered nature and one did not need a very keen perception to see its effects in the world at large. Augustine stands forth as a pessimist regarding humanity in the face of Pelagian optimism.

The Dangerous Extremes

The values themselves that underlie these two positions can of course be carried to dangerous extremes and thus become disvalues. Pelagius's emphasis on human freedom to obey seems to make God into a tyrant; and the autonomous response of the person to God does not appear softened by the dynamics of love. In this respect Pelagianism can be linked to the tradition of Stoicism. The key role of law and an overemphasis on it can easily degenerate into the very legalism that the Gospel is meant to overcome. And the elitism and perfectionism that Pelagius recommends seems so narrow that Christianity becomes either unrealistic or inhuman, or else the Church becomes an exclusive society hardly capable of accepting people into itself and breaking down the barriers that separate them. Pelagius wanted the whole Church to live the ascetic lives of monks. And, finally, the burden he places on freedom and autonomy is immense; Christianity ceases to be liberating and becomes terrifying.

The dangers of Augustine's position are more subtle but just as real. His doctrine of predestination cannot fail to be discouraging. Ultimately it offends not only human sensibility but also a Christian view of God. In the long run human autonomy is really compromised, the very autonomy that the Christian believes is established by God and guaranteed by his grace.

The Larger Issues

The case, however, cannot rest here, for each position had its consequences and has them still. Behind the Pelagian idealism one should not read naturalism; he believed in God's grace and the convert and the baptized person was different because of it.[8] And this is the point. Christian life was seen as a witness and sign of God and his grace to the pagan empire of this world. Pelagianism may stand for rigid asceticism or perfectionism; but the symbol should not distract from the issue of whether or not the Christian way of life is to be different in some degree, which, it seems, it must be if it is to be an effective sign at all of God's grace.

By contrast, Augustine's decisions seemed to favor a tolerance for Christian mediocrity. The Christian is essentially a "convalescent"; his life is saved, but he remains "sick."[9] Augustine's position allowed within the Church all the human failings that one finds outside it. And the effect was a leveling of the wholesale Christian witness to the common standard of the ordinary. This could only canonize the double standard of a nominal Christianity for ordinary people in the world and the "real" Christianity that led people to flee to the monasteries.

Intimately connected with the question of Christian anthropology, then, is the question of the Church. Pelagian emphasis on freedom should not be confused with individualism. Behind the Pelagian reform is a conception of the Church; Pelagius did not want the individual to be an ascetic outside the Church; he wanted the Church to become ascetic.[10] While this would be completely unreal in the context of a Church of the masses, a Church of "Christian Society," it is not so in a Church of the minority, a Church of the dedicated few. Pelagius was content with such; it was the ancient tradition. This issue suddenly becomes more real when it is realized that Christianity is now becoming more and more a Church of a conscious minority.

Augustine's view envisages the Church as the majority religion, the state Church, and the Church of the masses. Christianity swallowed the empire whole and introduced the Christendom of the Middle Ages. But as the Christendom consciousness breaks down it would seem that one has to ask whether the Augustinian decision in this regard was "cultural," that is, a spontaneous response that accorded with a historical movement, or whether it was a normatively Christian event. *Should* Christianity be the minority religion that it is rapidly becoming conscious of being?

A final issue regards the Christian judgment on the human history that unfolds outside the pale of explicit Christian revelation. Pelagian optimism can be translated into a positive view of that history. Even though, paradoxically, Pelagius recommended a rigid asceticism, he viewed human nature's freedom for the good as intact. By extension, such an interpretation leads one to accept the possibility of a human history that can be moving toward God without the help of explicit Christianity. In general Augustine was less sanguine about this world and its history. "To him earthly tasks could not have ultimate significance, for it was not easy to see how the building of the earthly city could make much difference to the final outcome."[11] For Augustine, grace is radically gratuitous "because it comes to a man who is sinful through and through, in no way deserving of the initiative by which God transforms his bad will into a good will."[12] "For Augustine, the good acts of pagans, though of some apparent value, are ultimately sham, because they do not bring pagans any closer to union with God."[13]

Two Symbols

Pelagius and Augustine were contemporary Christian leaders.
We have taken these two figures and expanded their religious experiences and views and doctrines into more and more general issues and
consequences. In the end one is left with two rather abstract but all-
embracing symbols that represent two opposing views of human existence, Christian life and Christianity itself. While these symbols remain abstract and general, they are not for all that detached from
life; they are rooted ultimately in the lives of those men who were
involved in definite moments of history, who both interpreted Paul,
but whose Christian experience generated very different ideas based
on fundamental values. They stand respectively for human autonomy and total dependency on God, for human freedom and the
constriction of that freedom so that it needs internal divine aid to
accomplish the good, for a universal possibility of salvation and an
optimistic view of human nature over against a pessimistic view of
human existence under the shadow of predestination.

Insofar as those symbols are abstract and general, they can be
considered as guides for thinking and questioning. The Pelagian controversy provides a splendid insight into the nature of human life and
Christian experience, and therefore it provides us with some basic
categories, heuristic concepts, with which one can see and analyze
tendencies in Christian thought and their dangerous extremes. One
must suppose that in such a fundamental question as was debated in
the Pelagian controversy, one that necessitated an authoritative decision of the Church, the elements and values at stake were "substantial," that is, implied in the very nature of Christian experience or
constitutive of Christian faith experience itself. And if this is so, the
opposing tendencies will be found to appear wherever Christian experience appears and in every understanding of it. The construction
of these symbols, then, by contrast and generalization, supplies types
by which one can see this structure in Christian experience in other
periods, in other understandings, and by which one can judge the
relevancy of past doctrinal assertions for today's Christian understanding. As a matter of fact, this is how the symbols of "Pelagianism" and "grace" in the Augustinian sense have always operated,
that is, as "critical" categories.

Treating the Pelagian controversy in this way obviously takes one beyond the study of the doctrinal formulas that mark its term, and in two ways: First, the analysis of the elements of the controversy takes one behind the doctrine, as it were, and by explaining its genesis gives one an understanding of what it means. And, second, it takes that doctrine itself not as a definitive term for understanding but as a point of departure for further understanding of the Christian experience. Doctrine is not an end, but a beginning for understanding.

One must suppose again that since each of the two symbols is evidently based on solid values, despite their excesses, aspects of each position must somehow be integrated into a total Christian view of man and the Christian life. If either of the symbolic positions espoused in Pelagianism and Augustinianism is taken by itself without the modifications that the other demands, if they are simply pitted against each other in an either/or fashion with no attempt at integration, one will inevitably be led to the untenable extremes that each position implies. This being the case, the symbols can be seen as poles of human life and Christian faith experience that must be integrated into Christian life and understanding. While the values of each must find a place in the Christian outlook, still, because they are opposing, they must be held in tension, one pulling against the other like the lines of force emanating from the two poles of one magnet. Because Christianity has unanimously judged that Augustine's is essentially the Christian doctrine, his view must provide the key to how this integration is to be effected, how the two poles will relate to one another. But, finally, before such a constructive synthesis can be attempted, certain problems with both the Pelagian and the Augustinian positions themselves must be criticized.

Ambiguous Assumptions

A number of the sometimes tacit, sometimes explicit assumptions of both Pelagius and Augustine are either questionable or at least can no longer be assumed today. Once these are laid bare, one is in a better position to see that the values that each position represents need not be opposed in such a way that they necessarily exclude each other.

Pelagianism's idea of freedom will not do. Freedom cannot be viewed simply as the power to choose; and the power to choose itself is not simply a purely detached or disinterested state of equilibrium by which persons can completely dispose of themselves either toward good or toward evil. Augustine's conception of the problem is considerably more profound and corresponds to some of the deepest experiences of the human person, especially today. There are levels in our life at which we are not in control of ourselves. And, moreover, human liberty and our elemental delight often seem twisted. This is both the personal experience of individuals and the experience of humankind in general. It is eminently attested to by Paul and what Paul Tillich calls "estranged existence." In whole areas of our existence we are passive to and a victim of our total self, our past and our milieu. Freud has vindicated Augustine on this point and so have the social sciences. The values, ideas and presuppositions, the prejudices and biases of society, do not remain simply external to us; they are internalized and shape us and thereby become inward determinants of our personality, of who we are. In short, the effects of both the determinisms of personality and the external attractions to sin are far deeper and more pervasive than Pelagianism supposes.

But, on the other hand, human freedom of choice is still an ideal and Augustine does not do it full justice. He too was working on a series of suppositions that must be modified. First, Augustine's conviction that infants who die without baptism are worthy of damnation can scarcely be admitted by Christians today. Such a doctrine offends common sense. This means, second, that Augustine's theory of Original Sin must be altered. In fact, the Pelagian theory would be much more plausible than Augustine's quasi-physical inheritance theory involving personal guilt if it were interpreted less extrinsically. Third, Christians today are much more willing to take the doctrine of the universal salvific will of God seriously. Augustine interpreted this doctrine particularistically, which means, in effect, that he interpreted it away.[14] Fourth, Augustine saw God's grace to the race as tied to closely to historical and explicit revelation. Again, Christians today are much more inclined to admit that God's grace is not merely coextensive with explicit revelation, the Church, or explicit faith. Explicit knowledge of Jesus Christ is not necessarily an ontological condition for grace's operating in any given individual or society, or in history at large. Theories of "anonymous" and "latent" Christianity are designed precisely to explain how grace may be operative universally. Fifth, Christians today are beginning to feel much more at home in the world and tend to think of Augustine's other-worldliness as escapist. Granted, no one has here a lasting city; still Christian life must be led in the world and it is being thought of more and more in terms of a life for this world. And sixth, Augustine seemed to confuse the absolute and total gratuity of grace with its nonuniversality. One need not say—indeed it seems difficult to say— that God's justice in punishing sin is needed to highlight his mercy in forgiving sin. There seems to be no contradiction to say—indeed, it seems more Christian to say—that while God's grace remains totally gratuitous, it is still operative in the life of every single human being. This last point is most important both for understanding Augustine and for any criticism of him. It is difficult to see how Augustine's doctrine of predestination can be distinguished from his vision of human nature and his doctrine of grace as some interpreters are inclined to do. This is no mere appendage; it is an essential and integral part of Augustine's conviction. And from this point of view it must be said that Augustine's people appear too dependent on God (if that can be said at all), that he ultimately robs human existence of its autonomy and compromises the Christian God in so doing. A way must be found in which the total gratuity of grace and the dependency of humanity on God are affirmed in a way that also preserves human autonomy or self-determination and our ability to freely respond to God as persons.

Integration through Polarity

More and more Christian theologians, especially existentialist theologians, are describing human existence as involving a fundamental ontological polarity. With this conception they are able to demythologize popular conceptions of the effects of Original Sin. Rahner views the division in human existence that is called concupiscence as the natural tension between "person" and "nature." Person corresponds to that center of human autonomy and freedom by which one asserts, posits and creates himself. On the other hand, nature represents human existence under the laws of our particular kind of being; the individual as conditioned, limited, finite, determined. What Rahner calls nature includes the whole of one's being insofar as it is *prior to* freedom and self-determination, and these "mechanisms" can be understood at a variety of levels, that is, biological, psychological, social, and so on. These two poles interact within human existence so that no one can ever be completely free of passivity, determinism, hindrances and obstacles to self-affirmation; free of desires, pushes and drives. People cannot "completely" determine themselves either for the good or for evil. But the more human beings transcend these spontaneous mechanisms and posit their whole self, sometimes against these a priori tendencies of nature, sometimes in the same direction, the more they become persons. Concupiscence is precisely this dualism, this tension between person and nature, especially insofar as it is an obstacle to performance of the good. Concupiscence is neutral; it is not sin; it only appears as concupiscence when it resists freedom and counters an individual's free disposition of the self toward the good. In short, concupiscence consists in the polar structure of actual human existence. There is an inner dualism within us, making us potentially divided selves, but within that dualism we strive for the ideal of unity and autonomy of personhood that comes with self-direction and self-positing.[15]

Tillich's description of the polar structure of "Freedom and Destiny" that is one of the constitutive elements of human being is remarkably similar to that of Rahner. Freedom and destiny are two elements existing together but pulling in opposite directions; they sustain each other by coexisting in dynamic tension, and as such they are a structure that constitutes human existence. To say that human existence is a polarity between freedom and unfreedom is to say that it is not a machine whose course is entirely predictable, on the one hand, and, on the other, that it is not a series of arbitrary acts. Freedom is exercised within a context of a whole series of systems and determinisms that are presupposed as the very matter to be assumed, directed and disposed by freedom. "Biological, psychological, and sociological powers are effective in every individual decision. The universe works through us as part of the universe."[16]

Freedom, Sin and Grace

If this polarity exists within us, if it constitutes an aspect of the very structure of human life and existence, it can serve as a framework for understanding how grace operates within the human personality. It is apparent that these poles roughly correspond to the Pelagian pole or symbol of freedom and the Augustinian pole or symbol of the constriction and inner paralysis of habit, custom and sin that demands God's assistance and help through grace. But it is Augustine himself who provides the more profound and satisfying view of human freedom and consequently of the relation of God's grace to it. Augustine's profound analysis allows one to see the working of grace on a much deeper level than that of the overt mechanics of external alternative and internal choice. Ultimately, to preserve both the role of grace and human freedom and autonomy one must conceive of grace as operating in human life in such a way as not to undermine that freedom, and this demands a relationship involving some sort of cooperation between God and human beings in the exercise of freedom and the doing of good. Here again Augustine provides the beginnings of an understanding when he says that grace does not destroy but establishes human freedom.[17]

There are several levels on which grace can be seen as establishing freedom and autonomy. In outlining these various levels we take Rahner's definition of grace as our guide: Grace is the self-donation of God to human beings. Grace means that God gives himself to individuals, is present to them, in a new and personal way. Moreover it is assumed that God's grace is present and available to everyone in some way because of God's universal salvific will.[18]

Grace Guarantees Human Autonomy

On a first and most fundamental level, God's grace can be seen as constituting human autonomy. This is more than an abstract statement of assertion of blind faith, for it corresponds to something that can enter into experience. To grasp what it means to say that grace establishes a person's autonomy the statement must be seen over against the negative aspects of finitude and the destructive forces of temporality, that is, of being unto death. In such a situation the personal address of an infinite and absolute God guarantees the autonomy of human existence over against these forces. In Augustine's terms, to be in contact with the One, the True and the Good is to share in the absoluteness of these qualities. Even while remaining dependent on God, the free address of God to human beings gives them an absoluteness and autonomy that they would not have and could never experience outside of this relationship. This is best expressed by Augustine when he says that a person desires to be, and to be absolutely means to be in God. "If you begin by wishing to exist, and add a desire for fuller and fuller existence, you rise in the scale, and are furnished for life that supremely is . . . . If you wish more and more to exist, you will draw near to him who exists supremely."[19] This desire for an autonomy of being is supremely fulfilled when it is met by the personal contact with God that grace mediates.

Grace Expands Freedom by Giving Liberty

Closely related to human autonomy in being is the exercise of autonomy in free self-determination. In the tension that governs human existence there is always the tendency for the individual as person to slip back into the determinisms that control his or her life. There is a force that is experienced as a law of least resistance by which people tend not to exert themselves, but to succumb passively to the mechanisms that structure the self, from within, from society, from the world. However, it does not seem that any concept of grace is necessary in order to understand how the freedom and personhood that is inherent in human existence can exercise itself against these forces. It would seem that Pelagius (and Rahner and Tillich) is correct in saying that this power is part of the very nature of humanity and no concept of grace is needed to explain the human ability to determine the self.[20]

There is, however, much more to be said and Augustine views the matter much more profoundly when he injects his distinction between freedom and liberty into the discussion. Freedom or free will (*librum arbitrium*) is the power to choose this or that; liberty (*libertas*) is the power to choose the transcendent good and stems from an inner "delight" in the good, which is a gift of the Holy Spirit, that is, grace.[21] "It is certain that it is we that *will* when we will, but it is He who makes us will what is good . . . . It is certain that it is we that act when we act; but it is He who makes us act, by applying efficacious powers to our will."[22] Without this grace the choices of human freedom are interiorly bound by concupiscence and by the inner bonds built up through habit and the custom of self-seeking. Thus in Augustine grace is seen as a force that expands the field or horizon of freedom to include the possibility of decision that transcends the self and this world in its intentionality. And again, this is no mere assertion, for it can be, as it was by Augustine, experienced in one's own life. The experience of being in contact with a transcendent and absolute God, the source and sustainer of all that is, and one who addresses us by personal gift and calling, draws the exercise of freedom beyond the limited and finite and ultimately disappearing values of this-world-taken-in-itself. This does not mean, however, that decisions in and for the values of this world are bypassed so that God becomes one's only motive for acting, as Augustine tended to think. Rather, what we are describing here is an entirely new dimension whereby decisions in and for this world are given a qualitatively different consistency precisely because they transpire in an entirely new context of the ultimately important and permanently valuable. It is not that concrete opportunities are numerically multiplied by this new liberty; it is rather that freedom is expanded because the objects of choice and decision exist in a new context of importance. In this way liberty expands freedom.

Viewed in connection with the first level of the operation of grace—that is, its function of constituting human autonomy and absoluteness—here contact with God through his grace enables a person to exert himself or herself over the determinisms of nature in a new and qualitatively different way, in an ultimate and absolutely meaningful way that would not be possible without this intimate contact with God. Viewing the matter psychologically, as Augustine himself does, by reorienting our elemental desire, interest and delight, as well as our understanding of being over which we have little control, the touch of grace not only reconstitutes our person but also our freedom of decision in a qualitatively new way; it gives "personhood" and its ability to posit the self an entirely new and absolute dimension. And this can in turn be translated into the concrete motivation and determination needed to pass into new forms of action.

Grace Overcomes the Roots of Sin

Still another and distinct level of the operation of grace has to do with sin. Some would incline toward identifying the human tendency to sin with the very mechanisms of nature, those forces that tend to submerge the transcending exercise of person and freedom in love.[23] While there is some truth in this, that is, that selfishness often implies taking the path of least resistance, still seeing this as the ultimate root of sin is to miss the depth of the Augustinian insight. It is true that Augustine made much of habit and custom imprisoning the will; but sin itself is much more than passivity and succumbing, and in itself it is much more than the determinisms that govern life. For Augustine, sin resides in the will itself and this is its mystery; sin is in human *freedom*; it passes through habit and custom to reside in the spiritual "person."[24] It is a *cupiditas* by which we *assert* ourselves but cannot transcend ourselves; one tries to draw reality into himself or herself. *Cupiditas* makes the individual precisely as person the norm and value of all other things and uses the world and the others to satisfy the self.

For Augustine, the effects of sin come to be lodged in the person, and it is here that the "medicinal" quality of grace is experienced. The personal contact with God through his grace reorients person; *cupiditas* becomes *caritas* or love, a love not only for the good as such but a love that recognizes that others have an absolute value in themselves and cannot be used as a means of self-satisfaction or as a means for anything. Love establishes a basic reverence that allows the other to be what it is in itself (himself or herself) and tends to foster that value. And this too need not remain an abstract assertion or arbitrary construct; it can be experienced and can be seen in the lives of the saints.

On those three levels, then, one can see how God's personal gift of himself to human beings can establish and guarantee human autonomy, can expand the horizon of freedom and personhood so that one can assert himself or herself in, through and above the passive elements of human nature with new quality and force, and, finally, can liberate human existence from the inner imprisoning force of egoism and selfishness. It should be insisted, however, that these three distinct levels of the operation of grace cannot really be separated. Although autonomy and personhood are values in themselves, if they are separated from the third level there will be a tendency to interpret religious experience and the operation of grace in terms of personal fulfillment or psychological wholeness and integrity. To see religious experience or religion simply as a means of mental health and an integrated personality is the most fundamental distortion possible, even though it is not uncommon.

Grace in the World Today

If grace is real, it must be experienced; if grace is a reality in the world, it must become manifest. And this "becoming visible" will be seen in terms of actually existing systems that destroy human autonomy and alienate persons by imprisoning freedom. To put the same thing negatively, if there are no movements within history where persons assert their own freedom and try to spread goodness by freeing others from the forces of alienation and depersonalization, the assertion that God's grace or God's Spirit is at work immanently in the world will seem sheerly arbitrary and gratuitous.

To understand the threat to human autonomy and freedom, which is guaranteed by God, one should not slip back into the spirit-matter dualism that was common in Augustine's time. The dualism, or, better, polar tension that Rahner and Tillich speak of is not that of pure spirit being threatened by the power of sensuality and the material world as if the material world were somehow evil or separate from spirit. Rather, the moral dualism or polarity in which autonomy, freedom and personhood are threatened should be envisaged in the concrete systems of reality that modern philosophy and science have disclosed. These are the mechanisms and determinisms that are biological, psychological, educational, social, cultural, economic, political, ideological. All of these are the determinisms of nature, which people can either passively "suffer" or actively transcend, by putting them in service of personhood, by bestowing on them something of an absolute value and meaning, by controlling them for human existence. God's grace, then, insofar as it is a force that liberates human existence, guarantees its autonomy and expands its freedom, should be seen as unfolding in this world in terms of these imprisoning factors. Its vehicle will be those human beings who in service of others attack and criticize the forces of dependence and alienation. "In other words: the economic alienation discussed by Marx and the psychological alienation discussed by Freud cannot be alien to the Christian conception of redemption."[25]

Since Augustine, the notion of grace as a medicinal force, as a sanative power of God releasing us from an internal bondage, especially of sin, has been a permanent fixture in the Christian language about grace. Although this theme probably plays a greater role in Protestant spirituality and talk about grace than in the Catholic, still it is a universal theme in the teaching of Western Christianity. And this corresponds not only to Pauline teaching but also to the deepest Christian experience of the freeing and liberation that Christ mediates to the believer. The grace of Christ constitutes human autonomy and expands human freedom giving it a new depth and power. And it overcomes the egoism and selfishness that is sin. This understanding of grace as a dynamic liberating force for freedom and action for the good remained the dominating conception of grace right up to the thirteenth century when, around the time of Aquinas, the understanding of grace underwent a dramatic shift.

This does not solve some of the wider issues that the Pelagian controversy raised. As Christianity shifts back today into the state of being in a self-conscious way the minority religion in the world that it was in the pre-Constantinian era, some basic questions are reopened, but on new and different suppositions from those shared in the time of Augustine. Moreover, if the Christian community begins to conceive of itself as a sign to the world and a mediator and sacramental presence of grace, then the whole question of Pelagian reform and "elitism," if only it can be stripped of its negative overtones, must also be rethought. Can Christianity still be thought of as the religion of the masses? And to what extent is much of our theology of the Church based on the tacit suppositions of a Christendom that can no longer exist?

Notes

1. Augustine, "To Simplician—On Various Questions," Bk. I, ques. 2, vii, 21, in *Augustine: Earlier Writings*, ed. and trans. John H. S. Burleigh (Philadelphia: Westminster Press, 1953), p. 405.

2. Eugene TeSelle, *Augustine the Theologian* (London: Burns and Oates, 1970), p. 182.

3. Augustine, *Confessions*, Bk. X, chap. 29.

4. Peter Brown, *Augustine of Hippo* (Berkeley: University of California Press, 1969), p. 179.

5. "They, who are not liberated through grace, either because they are

not able to hear, or because they are unwilling to obey; or again because they did not receive, at the time when they were unable on account of youth to hear, that bath of regeneration, which they might have received and through which they might have been saved, are indeed justly condemned; because they are not without sin, either that which they have derived from their birth, or that which they have added from their own misconduct" (Augustine, "On Nature and Grace," chap. 4 in *Basic Writings of Saint Augustine*, I, ed. Whitney Oates [New York: Random House, 1948], pp. 523–524). TeSelle believes that this doctrine of Original Sin and the necessity of baptism for an infant's salvation is very central to Augustine's thought, so much so that his narrow doctrine of predestination depended on it rather than on the theology of grace. Because some infants were baptized and others not, Augustine was forced to conclude to a strict predestination to salvation of some and not others, a predestination that seemed to be empirically verified (TeSelle, *Augustine the Theologian*, pp. 323–325).

6. Augustine, "On Grace and Free Will," chap. 44 in *Basic Writings of Saint Augustine*, I, p. 772.

7. Brown, *Augustine of Hippo*, p. 352.

8. Peter Brown, "Pelagius and His Supporters: Aims and Environment," *The Journal of Theological Studies* 19 (April 1968): 103.

9. Brown, *Augustine of Hippo*, p. 365; "Pelagius and His Supporters," pp. 110–111.

10. Brown, "Pelagius and His Supporters," pp. 102–103.

11. TeSelle, *Augustine the Theologian*, p. 271.

12. Jean-Marc LaPorte, "The Dynamics of Grace in Aquinas: A Structural Approach," *Theological Studies* 34 (June 1973): 222.

13. Ibid., p. 221. Cf. Augustine, "On the Spirit and the Letter," chap. 48, in *Basic Writings of Saint Augustine*, I, pp. 498–500.

14. TeSelle, *Augustine the Theologian*, pp. 319–320. Cf. Augustine, "On the Spirit and the Letter," chap. 40, pp. 491–492.

15. Karl Rahner, "The Theological Concept of Concupiscentia," *Theological Investigations* I (Baltimore: Helicon Press, 1961), pp. 347–382, esp. pp. 359–366.

16. Paul Tillich, *Systematic Theology*, II (Chicago: The University of Chicago Press, 1957), p. 42. Cf. also *Systematic Theology*, I, pp. 198–201.

17. Augustine, "On the Spirit and the Letter," chap. 52 in *Basic Writings of Saint Augustine*, pp. 503–504.

18. Cf. Karl Rahner, "Nature and Grace," *Theological Investigations* IV (Baltimore: Helicon Press, 1966), pp. 165–188.

19. Augustine, "On Free Will," Bk. III, vii, 21, in *Augustine: Earlier Writings*, p. 183.

20. A good portion of this interpretation is inspired by Juan Luis Segundo, *Grace and the Human Condition* (Maryknoll, N.Y.: Orbis Books, 1973), pp. 21–39, 43–46. However, this analysis differs somewhat and the levels outlined here seem confused in his presentation. Segundo wants to establish the fact that grace establishes freedom itself by giving "person" the

very power to posit itself over against the tendency of least resistance, of slipping back through nonexertion of self into mechanism and routine. But one does not need a concept of grace to explain the exercise of freedom as Pelagius explained and Augustine agreed.

21. Augustine, "On the Spirit and the Letter," chap. 28 in *Basic Writings of Saint Augustine*, I, p. 483.

22. Augustine, "On Grace and Free Will," chap. 32 in *Basic Writings of Saint Augustine*, pp. 759–760.

23. Segundo tends to identify sin with the mechanisms of nature to which a human being submits instead of exercising freedom and love against them. This identification of sin with mechanism is never complete, however, and obviously there is some connection between sin and the determinisms of life. But the more one leans toward that identification the more the mystery of sin is explained away. Sin and egoism are not passivity and ultimately not rooted in determinism. Sin is diminished when passivity and mechanism increase; and it increases when freedom and responsibility increase. This is precisely the problem with egoism; it is self-assertion and rooted in the will itself.

24. Cf. Augustine, *Confessions*, Bk. VIII, chap. 8 and chap. 10, where he depicts the will as prisoner to itself.

25. Segundo, *Grace*, p. 35. Cf. also pp. 32–35. In chap. 8 we shall return to this theme in a fuller, more constructive discussion.

3
Aquinas: Nature and Grace

In representing in a summary way the contribution of Aquinas to the theology of grace any number of perspectives might be chosen. The intention here is quite explicitly to highlight the difference between the Scholastic understanding of grace and that of Augustine. There are always disadvantages in choosing a definite and limited perspective. But in this case the disadvantages do not include losing sight of continuity in the theology of grace. For precisely in the contrast and dramatic shift in the theology of grace that Aquinas represents, the continuing presence of Augustinian themes in his theology stands out all the more sharply.

The basic question that underlies the following interpretation is this: What happened to the language of grace in the Scholastic period, and particularly in Aquinas? In general, what happened is the result of the influence of "The Philosopher," Aristotle. And so quite naturally one should begin with the rise of Aristotelianism in the West, and the revolution it wrought in theological method and understanding.

The Arrival of Aristotle
At the age of about thirteen or fourteen years, Tomaso d'Aquino was taken out of the Benedictine monastery at Monte Cassino to continue his studies at the recently founded university in Naples. The transition is symbolic. For education itself had been shifting for some time from the older monastery schools to city schools, and these had gradually evolved into universities, semiautonomous centers of learning located in the cities: at Bologna, at Oxford, at Montpellier, at

Toulouse, at Cologne, and so on. Theological education, which was the climax and crown of the university curriculum, had thus passed from a setting that was rural and isolated, that was stable and spiritual, to one that was international and highly professional. And the queen of all the university centers and universities was Paris. A convenient date for the founding of the University of Paris is 1200.

When Tomaso d'Aquino arrived at the University of Naples, approximately around the year 1239,[1] Aristotle was well known there. In fact, the greater part of Aristotle's writings were available for Latin readers by the year 1200.[2] But the impact of Aristotle, particularly his philosophy of nature, did not have its full effect until later on in the century and in a sense Aquinas would represent the fullest and most perfect integration of it into theology.

"The intellectual life of the thirteenth century," Van Steenberghen writes, "was dominated by one prime historical fact: the introduction into the West of an abundance of philosophical and scientific literature, Greek, Jewish and Arabian in origin, in successive waves from the mid-twelfth to the mid-thirteenth century."[3] Along with Aristotle, Avicenna, Averroes, Avicebron, Maimonides and others were being translated into Latin in centers like Toledo and Naples. Aristotle and his commentators represented a naturalistic view of the world. In them the world appeared with an internal consistency of its own. The cosmos was a hierarchy of beings having their own natures or intrinsic principles of intelligibility and operation, and the human mind could grasp these natures and classify them; it could understand the world in terms of its causes, interrelations and goals. On the one hand, the curiosity and inquisitiveness that this startling awareness unleashed, and the deep confidence that human reason could understand this world and that its processes corresponded to the laws of reasoning, and the precisions of conceptualization and reasoning that Aristotle's language and his logics provided—all these helped to transform theology into a scientific discipline. But on the other hand, Aristotle was greeted with deep suspicion, for his naturalistic outlook seemed to clash with the Christian view of reality as completely dependent on God. Christian consciousness was shocked because for it truth and wisdom came from God and was based on his authority as represented in the Scriptures, in the great Doctors like Augustine, and in the Church. Aristotle would be accepted only after many condemnations and bitter controversies, especially in Paris. Aquinas was probably able to stand firm and confident in his Aristotelianism because of his early familiarity with him, because of the later example of his teacher Albert, who more than any single person argued for the autonomous rights of learning and science, and because of his own studies, commentaries upon, and vast knowledge of "The Philosopher."

The Augustinian Tradition on Grace

The understanding of grace in Augustine is set against the background of Original Sin. To the question of the ultimate reason for the need of grace by human beings, the response was Original Sin and its effects on human subjects and human nature itself.[4]

In Augustine, the concept or idea of "nature" is concrete, existential and historical. For him, human nature usually stands for what human beings are at any given period of history. Nature can refer to the original condition of humanity, to pristine human being as it comes forth from the Creator, and thus to human existence as righteous, without sin and in grace. Nature in this usage includes the gifts of grace. But nature also refers to the condition of humanity after the Fall, and in this usage nature is deprived of grace so that the person in his or her natural state is filled with sinful tendencies. Thus nature in Augustine is not continuously identical; it is not an unchanging essential substance. To say that nature is historical, then, means that human nature changed with the historical Fall and is not now what it used to be.[5]

The problem of human nature in Augustine, moreover, is neatly focused on human will and its freedom. Because of the Pelagian controversy, the teaching of Augustine on grace became narrowed down to the context of sin and freedom. The problem of human nature is moral; it concerns what we can will and do that is pleasing to God. More precisely, the human problem is our sinfulness, the debility of our will, the fact that we cannot do good, that we cannot perform any meritorious action, that we cannot do anything in this our present state that is ultimately pleasing to God without grace.[6]

Grace is understood according to the context in which it is viewed; it tends to be defined in terms of the problem to which it responds. Thus, first of all, the gratuity of grace, which is close to the essence of the very meaning of grace, is seen as a function of human sinfulness in Augustine. Why is grace gratuitous? Why is grace grace? Why is it completely unmerited and freely given by God? The response is because of our now inherent sinfulness. Human beings need grace because of their godlessness, their evil will and behavior.[7]

Second, there is no clear, sharp distinction between the natural and the supernatural in Augustine, and certainly no dichotomy.[8] The term "supernatural" did not exist in Augustine's period and would not enter the theological world until the ninth century, after which it would fall out of use and reappear in the thirteenth. For Augustine, our actual nature, the way we are now, includes both a desire for what would later be called the supernatural and a refusal of it because of sin.[9] Here we see the roots in the actual nature of human existence for a potentially divided psychological self, one that is dramatically described in the *Confessions*, especially in the climax before decision presented in Book 8.

Third, it is because of the problematic of freedom and sin that grace appears in Augustine as essentially a divine force, power or influence within persons, reordering their nature and enabling them to effect the good. Grace corrects nature and restores it to what it should be. Grace is sanative, medicinal, healing. And perhaps most important of all, the effects of this force that is named the assistance of the Holy Spirit are set forth in descriptive, existential and psychological terms. Grace is described in terms of human motivation and behavior, in the language of desire and delight, intention and choice, willing and action.

This tradition of seeing grace as God acting in human subjects lasted right up into the thirteenth century. Augustine had taught that through faith one received the Holy Spirit and the virtue of charity that enabled a person to act with an ordered will, a will that desired the good as such. Peter Lombard, whose *Book of Sentences* was so important during the hundred years previous to Aquinas, taught that grace and the Holy Spirit and charity were all identical. He quoted Paul: "For the Love of God has been poured into our hearts by the Holy Spirit who has been given to us." (Rom. 5:5). Human virtue is virtuous action and that virtuous action is the direct result of grace or the Holy Spirit working in us. Grace is still conceived of as the force and power behind any virtuous or loving action human beings can perform, that is, any act of love. Grace is God acting in human existence, in persons.

The Shift in the Understanding of Grace

The change in the understanding of grace did not happen all at once. It is the product of a corporate effort of theologians who, in addressing various questions, gradually answered them by bringing to bear the newly introduced Aristotelian categories. Aquinas really marks the term of a transition that was negotiated all through the thirteenth century. In order to simplify and schematize that transition, it may be considered as hinging on two Aristotelian notions, that of nature and that of virtue.

In Augustine, grace is gratuitous because human beings are sinners. But the further question arises as to the deeper metaphysical ground of gratuity. Why, for example, is grace gratuitous in the case of Adam (or pristine human existence) who after all was not created a sinner? Here one is looking for the metaphysical reason why grace must be gratuitously given to human existence as such.

The answer to this question was mediated through the idea of nature in the Aristotelian sense of a metaphysical and substantive principle of being. Nature is the permanent principle of human being or being human; persons are human persons because of their nature of being human and this cannot change substantially. In short, nature is the principle that makes a thing what it is; it is the permanent ground that makes human beings human. Moreover, nature is also a principle of operation and activity that is teleological. Every being acts according to its nature and toward an end proportioned to it. And in the hierarchy of being and beings, God is infinitely above, or supernatural, in relation to human being. Therefore, the end to which human beings are called, that is, the spiritual union with God in knowledge and love that is made known by revelation alone, is supernatural in relation to human being and its nature. Thus human being needs a new and higher nature proportioned to its supernatural end in order to attain it: Even Adam needs grace because he is a finite creature and a human being. And this new nature is given in utter gratuity, in complete freedom on the part of God, since there is nothing in human nature that merits this elevation. This was the answer given by Philip the Chancellor around the year 1225. Laporte says that, in his writings, "grace is gratuitous because it is supernatural, because it brings man to a fulfillment over and beyond what the forces of his nature can achieve."[10]

As a result, grace began to be conceived of in a radically new way. Grace is not gratuitous because of humanity's sin, but because of humanity's being, being human, and because human being or nature is ordained to an end that is radically transcendent to this nature. There is a radical distinction between the natural and the supernatural orders and grace appears as a new nature. The main reason why grace is needed is not the debility of human will or action; grace is needed as an elevation of human nature making it proportionate as a principle of being and acting to a supernatural end. The former stress on medicinal grace and forgiveness of sin, grace as a cure for the effects of Original Sin, yields to another center of concern and becomes itself a related question. Grace is discussed in an entirely new context that is ontological and cosmological. The discussion deals with the relation between a distinct and coherent natural order, which consits of beings having to a certain extent their own proper ends in a hierarchy of being, and a higher or supernatural order.[11]

Still another important transition in the thirteenth century theology of grace came with the introduction of the Aristotelian concept of habit. In Aristotle and Aquinas a virtue is a habit, and a habit is an interior quality and permanent disposition of the soul.[12] It is not an action or a movement; it is an immanent principle of movement and action. And just as there are inborn habits and dispositions, and acquired habits and virtues, so too there can be infused habits and virtues. But what is most important is that according to Aristotelian and Thomistic metaphysics, every act of a human being must be elicited through some form or habit as the immanent principle of that specific act; otherwise, it would not be an act of that person. This means that if God acted merely in me or for me or through me, the act would not be my act; for an act to be mine at all it must be elicited through me as a principle of operation. And this is an absolute metaphysical principle.[13]

In the Augustinian tradition, grace is both God acting in the person and the force of his influence in our psychology and action. But certain questions arise in connection with this. Is there such a thing as a permanent *state* of being-in-grace? What happens for example in the baptized infant who is incapable of an active response under the influence of grace? If an act of charity is God working in a person, in what sense is it meritorious as far as that person is concerned, or even an act of that person at all?

In response to the last question and on the basis of the metaphysical principle just mentioned, Aquinas argued against Lombard by proposing a dilemma: If human acts of charity do not flow from and though an immanent and infused virtue within a person, the virtue of charity, then they will be the result of a natural virtue and will not surpass nature. But this is heretical and against the doctrine of Augustine. Or else, these acts will not proceed at all from a principle or form immanent in the person, and in this case they will be neither voluntary nor meritorious acts; in fact, they will not be the acts of the person at all strictly speaking. Lombard's conception, when viewed in terms of Aristotelian principles, makes the person an instrument of the Spirit so that, in effect, acts of charity are not personal at all, and even do violence to human freedom.[14]

What then is grace and what is its relation to the virtues (primarily of faith, hope and charity) and the meritorious acts of a person under the influence of grace? Grace is conceived of as a habit, that is, as a form infused into the soul. As such it is a permanent quality or "disposition" that remains or perdures. Since a habit is a specific principle of operation, grace is conceived of as the new nature, the higher principle of activity oriented to a supernatural end. Thus the ideas of nature and habit merge. As for the virtues of faith, hope and charity, they too are habits or principles of operation that are rooted in grace as their foundation, and that qualify the faculties of a person as virtues, faith and hope modifying the intellect, and charity the will. In this way, Augustine's understanding of grace, his psychological description of human existence in need of grace to perform free and good action, is assumed into Aquinas's Aristotelian system and subordinated to an ontological structure in which human nature is raised up by a "new nature" in which the virtues are grounded as permanent dispositions for action. Grace is understood by its being inserted analogously into an intelligible pattern of being.

Aquinas understood the structure of a graced person as running parallel to the structure of Aristotle's human nature, that is, a specific nature, whose acts are oriented and proportioned to a definite goal. "There finally resulted the systematization that we are familiar with: Grace is a new nature in which the infused virutes—especially faith, hope and charity—are rooted as proximate principles of our supernatural acts [acts oriented and proportioned to our supernatual end]."[15]

Grace in the Augustinian tradition was healing, sanative, medicinal; it sraightened out human motivation and will. Grace is still healing in Aquinas, but this is not described in psychological terms at all. Grace does not primarily heal human will or desire; rather, it heals human nature. Ontologically, human nature cannot even accomplish its own natural end; grace heals it (or better, raises it up) ontologically by enabling it to fulfill the whole good that is connatural to it (*ST,* I–II, 109, 2). Habitual grace, then, is not simply a new nature ordained to a supernatural end—it is also an ontological healing; this new principle of activity is needed both to raise up finite nature *and* to heal a fallen nature. Thus, not only is the dimension of a new nature for a supernatural end added to the notion of grace, but also the whole past history of grace as a movement that heals is subsumed into this ontological perspective.

Grace in Aquinas

Viewing the matter functionally, grace in Aquinas is before all else *elevating*. This is the primary need in human nature and the primary role that grace fulfills according to the logic of viewing human existence as nature oriented to an end that transcends its created force and capacity. It should be noted that grace is not elevating because of experiential reasons, even though experience can be cited that corresponds to the assertion, but because grace is inserted into a system in which the end of human existence is seen as absolutely transcending human nature and its proportionate power of activity so that a new elevating nature is required proportionate to that supernatural end (*ST,* I–II, 109, 2; I–II, 112, 1). In other words, within a system in which nature is viewed as having an end of its own other than the end to which Christian life is called, grace introduces a new end and therefore an elevation. Grace is elevating because of the integrity of nature, that is, the naturalism which Aquinas accepts from Aristotle.

Second, grace in Aquinas, ontologically speaking, is a *habit*. The word "grace" is reserved in his writings for "habitual grace." This means that grace is a permanent disposition residing in the human spirit. "Grace is reduced to the first kind of quality [i.e., 'a habit or disposition']. However it is not simply a virtue; rather it is a kind of habitual state which is presupposed by the infused virtues, as their origin and root" (*ST*, I–II, 110, 3, ad 3). But this does not mean that grace is a static and inert quality. The very act of God's infusing grace into the soul is a motion, movement and force so that even while grace from one point of view is a permanent elevating habit, from the point of view of its being infused in the human person it can be considered a movement within the personality (*ST*, I–II, 109, 9, ad 2).[16]

Third, because grace is a habit, it is, again ontologically speaking, a *quality* and an *accident*. Grace is a kind of being in the spirit of a person and since it is a kind of being it should be able to be described analogously in the categories of Aristotle. Grace is not a substance; it is rather an accident whose being is a being-in-another. Technically grace is a quality modifying the human spirit as a form or habit or dispostion. One must be very careful here not to allow the imagination to make grace into *a being*. It is not some*thing*. Rather it makes human being be or exist in a different way. Grace, by modifying the spirit, makes a person exist differently (Cf. ST, I–II, 110, 2, and ad 3).

Fourth, then, grace is *created*. Since grace inheres in the human spirit, since it is a form of the soul, grace is a created kind of being. It is for this reason that the term "created grace" became common in Scholasticism. Created grace is what Aquinas properly means when he uses the word grace, for created grace is identical with "elevating grace" and habitual grace. The term created grace simply highlights the fact that grace is something real within the human soul. In later Scholasticism, created grace came to be seen in opposition to "uncreated grace," which is the power and love of God himself communicating created grace. Again, created grace is not a thing; it comes to be or ceases to be insofar as its subject, the human person, is or is not in the mode or form of it under the influence of God (*ST*, I–II, 110, 2, and ad 3).

Fifth, grace, the habitual quality that raises human nature so that a person's activity may be proportionate to his or her transcendent end, is effectively a *new nature*. It is "a gratuitous capacity supplementing the capacity of his nature . . . to perform and will the supernatural good" (*ST*, I–II, 109, 2; cf. also I–II, 112, 1). The fundamental logic of the necessity of grace rests on the notion of teleology. Once human existence is considered as a nature, as oriented to a supernatural end to which this nature must be proportioned, it becomes apparent that human nature, that is, our very being as a principle of operation, must be raised if that transcendent end is to be reached. The habitual quality that raises human nature to the level of the gratuitously offered goal of humanity is thus a new nature.

Sixth, grace is *supernatural*. God is not supernatural in himself; he is simply the infinite and transcendent being; he is God. But viewed in relation to the human he is supernatural; that is to say, spiritual union with God transcends human nature and all its dynamisms absolutely. The first meaning of "supernatural," then, is "utterly transcendent to the human and everything finite." But the end of human existence as known through revelation is personal union with God, a spiritual "possession" in knowledge and love. Since there is an infinite and absolute distance between that end and human power or nature, human nature must be supplemented with a power or capacity proportionate to an end that infinitely transcends it and is added to it. There is a tendency today to reduce the idea contained in the word "supernatural" to gratuity.[17] This contemporary understanding is correct. But in *Aquinas* this cannot be said. Supernaturality is not simply gratuity; it is also the reason for gratuity, that is, the utter transcendence of God *in relation to human nature*. The idea of the supernatural depends on a concept of nature that is in itself closed to the end of human existence promised in Christianity. Thus one cannot escape, in Aquinas at least, the idea of something that must be added to nature. Human nature is insufficient for its *de facto* end; human existence needs another and a new nature, and this augments, or is added to, human nature and being.

Seventh, grace is absolutely *gratuitous*. The ultimate reason for this gratuity is that the end to which human existence is called utterly transcends its own proper nature. It should be noted that in Aristotelian-Thomistic metaphysics the proportion between nature and end has the quality of an intrinsic determination and is characterized by necessity. Moreover, Aquinas is very Greek in presupposing an immutable and immutably consistent Creator-God. On these suppositions, to affirm that human existence is oriented by its very nature toward a personal and spiritual possession of God as its proper object would imply either necessary universal salvation (which seems to offend God's justice) or an inconsistency in the Creator (if some persons do not reach this end). For this reason, the call to union with God is conceived of as utterly supernatural and therefore offered to persons with complete freedom by God. It should be noted that the reason for the gratuity of grace is no longer human sinfulness as in Augustine. But at the same time, the existential and historical character of human nature is *preserved* in Aquinas in the concepts of "intact" and "spoiled" nature and in the fact that we need grace even to fulfill the whole good that is natural to us (*ST*, I–II, 109, 2). But this understanding is subordinated to the metaphysical-ontological conception of nature.

Eighth, grace is also *justifying*. Justification is the process of passing from the state of sin to the state of righteousness or right order before God, a right relation to God. Aquinas conceives of this transition according to the model of "generation," that is, the coming into being of a new kind of being, or a new being or substance. Generation occurs when a being acquires a new substantial form, or when matter receives substantial form for the first time. Matter that was determined by form and constituted one being (or kind of being) becomes another being (or kind of being) when a new substantial form replaces the old. This model can be seen in Aquinas's description of justification (*ST*, I-II, 113, 1 and 7). On the analogy, the human soul is conceived of as the matter that receives a new form, that is, habitual grace.[18]

By the infusion of grace, a new quality of being, a new form or habit determining the human soul, a person passes from one state of being to another state of being. The process includes God's forgiving our sins. The end of the process, or the term of justification, is that a person exists in a new state of being. The person, in short, is sanctified.

And, finally, grace is *sanctifying*. The meaning of the sanctifying and divinizing function of grace is best seen in terms of another concept that Aquinas borrows from Greek philosophy, this time from the Platonic tradition, the idea of participation. Of this, Kenny writes:

> Life, knowledge, love, beauty, as found in creatures, are analogical participations of these attributes as they exist in God. Through participation in the created order there occurs no formal divine self-communication. But this is precisely what supernatural participation involves, which, consequently, is for St. Thomas the highest possible participation affecting created reality. Through it, the godhead, which belongs to God in an essential way, is communicated to creatures in an accidental way. In so far as it implies a formal sharing in the godhead itself, supernatural participation must be singled out from all other sorts.[19]

Grace, then, this created habit inhering in the soul, is a participation in God. Aquinas says that it is a participation in the goodness of God. Moreover, he says, it is a participation in the very nature of God. Through grace we participate in the life of God himself. In this way, elevating grace is also sanctifying (*ST,* I–II, 110, 1; I–II, 110, 2, ad 2; I–II, 110, 3; I–II, 112, 1). Because the divine life of God in human beings is not natural to them, it is not part of a person's substantial nature. It can only be something accidental and not essential to us, and so Aquinas emphasizes that grace is an accidental form in the soul (*ST,* I–II, 110, 2, ad 2). It should be noted here that there is a very strong emphasis in Aquinas on the real effect that God's love for human beings has on them. With the notion of participation and the notion of grace as a real mode of being of and in the human person, great weight is placed on the fact that the graced persons are really sanctified; that they really possess God's love as their own, so to speak; that their mode of being is radically changed and elevated into the divine life (Cf. *ST,* I–II, 110, 1). This is part of the force of the idea of created grace; it becomes something real in human existence itself even while it remains utterly gratuitous and "given," and a participation in what is entirely other, that is, God's life.

Conversion

The question of the process of justification brings up the basic Augustinian questions of preparation in a person for the reception of grace, that is, the turning to faith, conversion, merit and predestination. On all of these questions, Aquinas scarcely departs from basic Augustinian doctrine.

There must be a preparation in a person for the reception of grace because human existence is conscious and free and God must move persons, draw them to faith and grace, in a manner that respects that freedom (*ST*, I–II, 113, 3 and 7, ad 1). But this preparation on the part of a person is considered by Aquinas as a kind of *cooperation* with God's grace. There is no preparation in persons by their own power, no preparation that God himself does not supply. There is no self-preparation on the part of a human being before a divine movement moves this person toward the good. Thus the principal cause of the human preparation for justification is God, who moves human will; preparation is the movement of the free will of a person moved by God (*ST*, I–II, 112, 2 and ad 3).[20]

The movement on the part of a given person toward faith and grace, together with every meritorious act of that person, is conceived by Aquinas as a kind of cooperation. First of all, God gives the form or habit by which a person elicits an act that is meritorious or supernatural. If God does not infuse a form or habit—of faith, for example—there can be no supernatural act of faith. There can be no act of charity or love of God, no act of turning toward God that is salvific, without a supernatural form elevating a human act to a supernatural level. This principle is absolute, and it applies to every act leading to grace and salvation as well as every meritorious act performed in grace.[21] And second, God moves human beings to pass into act, but this second dependence is not strictly speaking supernatural in itself. All things depend for their movement on the first mover, God. *All* action and movement ultimately depends on God for its being set into movement (*ST*, I–II, 109, 1). Summarizing this cooperation, Bouillard says: "Man prepares himself by acts that are his; it is God who prepares him by infused habits. The act of faith proceeds at the same time from man and from God: from man insofar as it is a free act, from God (through the habit) insofar as it is a supernatural act. But it is as a *free act* that it constitutes a preparation or cooperation of man."[22]

Is there a preparation for grace through natural acts, one that, although imperfect, occurs before faith? Aquinas did admit that there was such a preparation in his earlier works, even though he held them to be radically insufficient to merit faith and grace. But in the *Summa,* he admits this no longer.[23] There is no place in the *Summa* for a remote preparation for faith and grace through the lights of reason or natural good will. "Conversion to God strictly begins with faith; and faith is in every respect a prevenient grace, an absolutely gratuitous gift of God."[24] Regarding those outside the realm of explicit revelation, Aquinas says that natural knowledge does not suffice for justification; people cannot convert themselves to God as the object of their beatitude (*ST*, I–II, 113, 4 ad 2). Ignorance of the truths necessary for salvation makes justification impossible (*ST*, II–II, 10, 1).

Thus Aquinas does not differ greatly in the *Summa* from Augustine on predestination. Everything within human nature that ordains a person toward salvation is subsumed under the title of predestination, including preparation for grace. As far as the effects of predestination are concerned, their ultimate reason is the divine will; by the divine will every effect of predestination is ordained to its end and proceeds as from its first cause. Why has God chosen these and not others for divine glory? There is no other ultimate reason than simply the will of God (*ST*, I, 23, 5 and ad 3).[25]

The Influence of Aquinas

It is certainly not the desire for a description of grace that appeals to our experience that generates an interest in Thomas Aquinas. A historical investigation into his thought on grace must be justified by other considerations, such as the historical genesis of his thought, its structure and systematic qualities, its content, and especially the influence it had. To understand a system of ideas such as Aquinas's, one must understand its genesis. The determining factor in thirteenth-century theology and in Aquinas is the rise of Aristotelianism. And like every other historical event, this one shares a note of arbitrariness. Why is it that Plotinus, who so influenced Augustine, was relatively unknown in the thirteenth century, and the Aristotle who so influenced Aquinas relatively unknown to Augustine? The irony is that a movement of thought that seemed at first so offensive to the Christian outlook, that was judged innovative, that was greeted with initial rejection and repeated condemnation by the Church, should become something like an absolute language for Roman Catholic faith for seven hundred years.

An appreciation of the qualities of Aquinas's language helps to explain how this happened. The discovery of Aristotle provided theologians like Aquinas both with the conceptual tools and the confidence in reason that enabled them to write such all-encompassing syntheses of "Sacred Doctrine" as the *Summa Theologiae*. In Aquinas's *Summa*, one sees an effort to make theology "scientific" in a way analogous to the science of Aristotle. The very abstractness and precision of Aquinas's language and the principles that underlie it, the rigid systematic and unvarying external form of the *Summa*, and its vast comprehensiveness, all make it appear as if the whole of Sacred Doctrine is contained in its three volumes. Although on closer examination there may be inconsistency and ambiguity in Aquinas's terminology, still, the overall achievement of a systematic and scientific theology, in the clear categories of Aristotelian natural philosophy, make the Scholastic synthesis appear like something complete and perennial.

In very general terms, moreover, Aquinas exemplifies the very nature of theology. It is an attempt at an appropriation of faith's content in coherent terms, and an articulation of affirmations about it. Aquinas typifies in a sense what the whole Scholastic period represents, that still valid ideal of theology, the attempt to think through and understand the content of faith—*fides quaerens intellectum*. One sees clearly in Aquinas that theology is not faith, but the attempt to understand it. And although many of the presuppositions of Aquinas's particular methodology are no longer tenable today, still his particular ideal is one of lasting value, namely, the confrontation of faith and reason. On the one hand, he receives through faith and from its positive sources in Scripture, the creed and the Fathers the data on which he reflects. But on the other hand, this is not a purely passive reception, for he tries to understand these data in the categories of reason that his period provides him with. Thus, in the process, the whole world of Aristotle is equally transformed by Christian faith and principles.

Otto Pesch calls Aquinas's theology "sapiential theology," a phrase that corresponds quite closely to scientific theology, that is, Aquinas's view of theology as the science of Sacred Doctrine. It is a quest for wisdom in the medieval sense of understanding a matter through its ultimate causes. Its categories are thus ontological, categories of being and the principles of being. Faith is the *basis* of its statements, but in the sense that one accepts the sources of revelation and their authority and then works from there. Each statement is not a function of an act of faith or of a religious experience. Thus this theology tends to be objective in the sense that faith is not active or thematized in every statement. It tends to be an objective description of reality out there; it is less confessional and speaks of God in the third person. This accounts for the marked difference between Aquinas and Augustine, as well as between Aquinas and Luther.[26]

Aquinas marks the peak of high Scholasticism. And the importance of the influence of Scholasticism, and of Aquinas's thought in particular, in determining the Roman Catholic language about grace cannot be overemphasized. Most of the basic doctrines of the Catholic Church are framed in the language of Scholasticism and for many Aquinas was *the* Scholastic and *the* Catholic theologian. Thus many of our common appreciations of grace are rooted in the little treatise on grace in the *Summa Theologiae*. Since the sixteenth century, Scholastic theology formed its understanding of grace in terms of the *Summa* and most manuals took their form from Aquinas. And although his was not the only theological influence and tradition within Scholasticism, it was the strongest.

Critical Observations

The critical remarks offered here are put forward with qualifications. As was said, Aquinas admirably illustrates the nature of theology as an attempt to understand the faith. And his synthesis was a giant achievement; few if any in the history of Christian thought have had comparable influence. But with the distance and the test that time has provided, and from the vantage point of contemporary experience and theology, certain precise criticisms can be brought to bear. But these criticisms are directed more against Scholasticism itself, of which Aquinas is probably the best representative, than against Aquinas. The following suggestions are not internal to the system, but criticism of the system itself. And they are offered from another context for understanding grace, one that is more experiential and articulated in personalist terms.

The first criticism of Scholastic theology and language is that it tends to become more and more divorced from experience. Historically this is symbolically represented by the move of theology from the atmosphere of the practical piety of the monastery environment into academic centers that became more and more fascinated with Aristotelian science. It is seen symbolically also in the rise of the *quaestio* for disputation in which points become more and more isolated from the *lectio* of Scripture and the Fathers to become problems in themselves. On the one hand, the disputation of questions was a dramatic breakthough in theology, for theologians could be seen actively theologizing; with less reliance on mere citation of past positions or of authority, they creatively thought through the further implications of faith in the light of new questions. But on the other hand, to the extent that the method of questioning and dialectic took on a life of its own, theology tended to be carried away into points more esoteric and divorced from real-life experience.

Chenu takes pains to point out that this tendency and danger are written into the very method and language itself of Scholasticism.[27] The method of abstraction by which it achieved its scientific precision and clarity, its dialectical versatility and technical machinery, its concern for external form, the endless classification, division, distinction and subdistinction, all made Scholasticism tend to drift away from experience into a world of its own.

An example of this in Aquinas's treatise on grace is seen in his treatment of the process of justification (Cf. *ST,* I–II, 113, 2–6). On the one hand, justification is considered as essentially a single act occurring in a moment of time on the model of physical generation

(I–II, 113, 6, ad 2). And on the other, it is broken down into its logical moments, its beginning, intermediary steps, and its term, and each is distinguished from the other by sheerly logical distinctions. When Aquinas treats the divisions of grace, grace becomes classified as prevenient or consequent again on the basis of logical points of view (*ST* I—II, 111, 3 and ad 2). In short, the whole interior and conscious drama of a conversion is not analyzed in its psychological stages of development. Rather, the single moment of passage into grace is divided up into moments that can be isolated logically and clearly distinguished from each other sheerly on the basis of abstraction.[28]

A second criticism of Aquinas's theological language about grace is much more fundamental. It concerns the propriety itself of his theological categories in connection with the mystery of grace. Is scientific and ontological language fitting and apt to express the central Christian mystery of grace? While recognizing that one must have some view of the relationship between the world and God, and between God and human nature, still it seems that these objective, scientific and ontological categories distort the relationship between God and human beings by placing it in a wider impersonal context. This question of the propriety of language is very delicate, but at the same time essential. When God offers people his grace, he enters into an interpersonal relationship with them. But this profoundly personal gift of God of his own love is drawn off center when placed in the context of an understanding that is framed in the objective ontological terms of nature and the elements of being. The categories of themselves subordinate this unique interpersonal and dialogic relationship to a wider and impersonal God-world context. For this reason it is being suggested today that the Christian mystery of grace must be approached in the personalist categories of encounter and intersubjectivity. Moreover, it has been said that the science of psychology might provide the analogies for the understanding of this relationship.[29]

An example of how metaphysical-ontological language can distort the love relationship between God and human existence that is grace is seen in Aquinas's treatment of conversion and justification according to the model of the generation of a new substance (*ST,* I–II, 113, 7). According to this paradigm, the process of justification is considered as instantaneous and the states of being-in-grace and not-being-in-grace are seen as simply contradictory and mutually exclusive. One has grace or one does not have grace; there can be no middle term. By thus understanding the process of the winning of a human personality to God's love by God's love in the terms of the generation of a substance, Aquinas has almost reduced it to mechanical terms. This is a fundamental distortion of the dynamics of grace when it is seen contrasted with a personalist description, and it has had enormous consequences in the history of the conception of grace. One has only to think of the seemingly mechanical loss and gain through sin and confession that has characterized popular conceptions in Catholic spirituality.

Third, there is a problem today with the word supernatural. To appreciate this problem it must be realized that words naturally tend to take on a life of their own and to react on human knowing by forming our consciousness. Added to this is the problem that occurs when a highly technical language such as that of Scholasticism is used as the common language of doctrine, instruction and catechisms, as happened in Catholicism. What is being described here, then, is a shift of consciousness and outlook that actually occurred and that is bound up with the word supernatural.

While admittedly the word supernatural may be taken as simply a code word for the transcendence of God and the utter gratuity of the gift of his personal love, still it also carries with it the idea of something *added on* to nature. This much is apparent from the study of Aquinas. But the word has gained still more connotations. The supernatural seems to come purely from the outside, from a God above history, almost arbitrarily, with only some people being its passive recipients. The new life of grace thus seems to be extrinsic to human existence itself and superimposed on nature. Should this be the case, it is difficult for human beings who are very concerned with this life and how it should be lived to see just how grace helps with *this* task. Grace seems irrelevant to human existence in this world precisely to the extent that it is supernatural, and the question arises of why human beings in their strictly human nature should not be indifferent to it. Moreover, if the very sharp distinction between what is natural and supernatural slides into a *separation* between these two orders, as is easily the case, other separations naturally follow; between religious life and temporal "natural" life; between the Church and the world; between salvation history and the rest of world history. However transcendent and gratuitous grace must be, it is for human beings now and in this world; it is God's immanence and presence to human existence in this life, and the *word* supernatural tends to obscure this fact.

Nature and Grace in Aquinas

We began this chapter with the question, What happened to the notion of grace in Aquinas's theology? We might conclude with a contrast between the notion of grace in Augustine and Aquinas. That contrast can be summed up in one sharp statement thus: Instead of being understood as the power and force of God working in human personality, in a person's willing and action, grace began to be thought of in the technical metaphysical and ontological categories of nature and habit. Grace had been understood in a moral context, in relation to the sin involved in human existence; in Aquinas grace is viewed ontologically within the context of simply being or being human. In this transition all the basic doctrines of Augustine were preserved; the working of God in human beings is not denied in Aquinas; it is explicitly provided for in his understanding. But the new cosmological context for understanding grace quickly subordinated the problematic of Augustine and when it was resurrected in the Reformation period it clashed with Scholastic understanding. Most important, with the context the whole language of grace shifted away from existential language that described grace working as a force in human life and history toward the abstract, technical and static language of being. The language of grace prescinded from religious experience.

As Scholasticism perdured, the supernatural realm more and more appeared as a sphere of existence that was utterly distinct from the natural and laid on top of it. Grace did not restore nature to what it should be; grace was added to nature. And because grace was still conceived of as intimately bound to and coextensive with the explicit knowledge of revelation, the world and its history seemed divided into two, the secular and the profane. Moreover, the logic of the Aristotelian naturalism and Thomistic supernaturalism that is contained in Scholasticism would leave theologians this unresolved dilemma: Either human nature, that is, human being itself, had a natural desire for the supernatural or it did not. If it did, the logic of nature's necessary proportion to its end would undermine the gratuity of grace. If it did not, then it would be hard to see why human beings, who tended to be looked upon as a "pure nature" existing in the autonomous and closed systems of the world, should need, desire or be interested in the world of supernatures at all while in this world.

What then can be said of the problem of the relationship between nature and grace? According to Eugene TeSelle, grace must be considered at three points:

1. At its origin, grace is the favor of God toward men, a free decision of love on their behalf.
2. Grace is also the communication of this divine decision to men, whether the emphasis falls upon historical events (as in much of modern theology), or upon the human words whose content is heard as revelation and thus becomes the power of God for salvation (as in classical Protestantism), or upon a special influence by which God acts inwardly upon men (as is usual in Catholic theology). Whatever the means may be, the original divine decision is effectively communicated to man.
3. Considered at its goal, grace is viewed as the foundation of a new relationship of man with God, and, however differently man's life under grace may be understood, in all cases it is viewed as the intended aim of the divine decision and its communication to man.

The crucial point of the distinction between nature and grace, TeSelle concludes, is that "grace opens up a possibility which does not lie within the scope of man's natural powers and is not implied by his being as a man." This distinction becomes necessary "when grace is understood as not implied by man's humanity as such."[30] This last point is the contribution of thirteenth-century theology as it is represented in Aquinas. The validity of this supernaturalist language of grace, however, is dependent on the naturalism it presupposes. Once a closed system of natures with immanent and proportioned goals gives way to one in which nature and human existence are seen as radically open, to an indefinite future and even an infinite goal, the concept of the supernatural may be discarded even as the notion of utter gratuity must be retained.[31]

Notes

1. These dates in the life of Aquinas are approximate, as is the estimated date of his birth in 1225. Cf. Angelus Walz, *Saint Thomas Aquinas: A Biographical Study* (Westminster, Md.: The Newman Press, 1951), pp. 1–27; Vernon J. Bourke, *Aquinas' Search for Wisdom* (Milwaukee: Bruce Publishing Co., 1965).

2. Fernand Van Steenberghen, *Aristotle in the West*, trans. Leonard Johnston (Louvain: E. Nauwelaerts, 1955), p. 62.

3. Ibid., p. 44.

4. There are other themes concerning grace in Augustine's writings, as for example, the idea of divinization. But because of the Pelagian controversy, the influence of Augustine's teaching on grace was narrowed into this line of thought.

5. Cf. Eugene TeSelle, *Augustine the Theologian* (London: Burns and Oates, 1970), pp. 289–290; Henri Rondet, *The Grace of Christ*, trans. Tad Guzie (New York: Newman Press, 1967), p. 204.

6. TeSelle, *Augustine the Theologian*, pp. 290–291; Rondet, *The Grace of Christ*, p. 204.

7. Jean-Marc Laporte, "The Dynamics of Grace in Aquinas: A Structural Approach," *Theological Studies* 24 (June 1973): 222. There are exceptions to this view in Augustine. When pushed by the Pelagian problematic, he too affirmed that even Adam, that is, human existence in its pristine and ideal state, would need the active force or assistance of grace to respond to God in love because such an act is beyond human [that is, "natural" in a certain "metaphysical" sense] powers (Augustine, "On Rebuke and Grace," chap. xxxxi–xxxii, in *The Works of Aurelius Augustine*, vol. XV, *The Anti-Pelagian Works of St. Augustine*, vol. III [Edinburgh: T. & T. Clark, 1876], pp. 99–101. See also "Nature and Grace," chap. 16, *The Basic Writings of Saint Augustine*, I, ed. Whitney Oates [New York: Random House, 1948], p. 557.) It is important to note, however, that while Aquinas will take his point of departure from the incapacity of human nature, Augustine was viewing Adam's human nature from the point of view of freedom, action and perseverance in the state of original goodness in which it was created. Although the assertions are similar, the context of Aquinas will be different and Augustine's thought cannot be simply reduced to that of Aquinas, especially relative to the category of the supernatural. See

Nigel Abercrombie, *The Origins of Jansenism* (Oxford: Clarendon Press, 1936), pp. 5–8.

8. See note 7 immediately above. Some interpreters tend to read the natural/supernatural distinction back into Augustine on the basis of human impotence, even when humanity existed in its ideal and graced state, to love God. This move is confusing since neither the terms nor the context of the later discussion are typically Augustinian. The point of Augustine is that all actions of love of God must be under the influence of divine love itself, that is, of the Holy Spirit.

9. Rondet, *The Grace of Christ,* p. 204.

10. Laporte, "The Dynamics of Grace in Aquinas," p. 223.

11. Cf. Rondet, *The Grace of Christ,* pp. 205–20. Cf. also, Aquinas, *Summa Theologiae,* I, q. 95, a. 4, ad 1 (hereafter referred to as *ST*).

12. Aquinas does distinguish between a habit and a virtue, because a virtue includes the note of perfection and therefore must include love or charity. But this distinction does not mark a difference of species or kind. Cf. *ST,* II–II, 4, 5, and ad 3.

13. *ST,* I–II, 109, 1 and 9; cf. also Henri Bouillard, *Conversion et grâce chez S. Thomas d'Aquin* (Paris: Aubier, Editions Montaigne, 1944), pp. 158–159.

14. Ibid., pp. 160–161, in connection with *ST,* II–II, 23, 2.

15. Rondet, *The Grace of Christ,* p. 201.

16. "Grace causes faith not only when faith begins anew to be in a man . . . God is always working man's justification, even as the sun is always lighting up the air" (*ST,* II–II, 4, 4, ad 3).

17. "*Supernatural* and *grace* are strictly synonyms, insofar as one is an adjective and the other is a noun. To put it better: supernatural adds nothing to the quality of gratuitousness which, as we saw it earlier, is the determining feature and content of the concept of grace. If grace signifies something given *gratis,* a gift, then supernatural signifies exactly the same thing—nothing more and nothing less. For it signifies what is added as a gift to the natural, that which does not belong to me by virtue of any right inherent in my nature as man" (Juan Luis Segundo, *Grace and the Human Condition* [Maryknoll, N.Y.: Orbis Books, 1973], p. 67).

18. Cf. Bouillard, *Conversion et grâce chez S. Thomas d'Aquin,* pp. 145–146.

19. J. P. Kenny, *The Supernatural* (New York: Alba House, 1972), p. 50.

20. Ibid., p. 148. We are avoiding the question here of whether or not there is a supernatural or elevating actual grace in Aquinas. This is a disputed question and there is evidence to support both contentions. By avoiding it, however, we are in a way taking sides with Bouillard who argues against such a notion in Aquinas. His basic argument is

from the consistency of the Thomistic synthesis; that is, the *auxilium Dei moventis* is intimately connected with the infusion itself of habitual grace and is not properly speaking a supernatural movement by God, but simply the dependence with which every act or movement is dependent on God for its very motion. Cf. esp. *ST,* I–II, 109, 1. Cf. also Bouillard, pp. 143–209, passim, but esp. pp. 173–209. For a counter position, see Bernard Lonergan, *Freedom and Grace* (New York: Herder and Herder, 1971).

21. An imperfect preparation for grace is possible, that is, acts of supernatural faith, performed through an infused habit of faith, but which do not come to term in conversion and grace. To explain this, one must recall that Aquinas envisaged the possibility of a habit of faith being given to a person without charity or sanctifying grace. Cf. *ST,* II–II, 4, 2–4.

22. Bouillard, *Conversion et grace chez S. Thomas D'Aquin,* p. 195.

23. Ibid., p. 190.

24. Ibid., p. 194. Aquinas owes his position here to Augustine and refers to him expressly in II–II, 2, 5, ad 1; II–II, 6, 1. This question of conversion is very closely linked with Pelagianism and more exactly with semi-Pelagianism. It involves the question of the gratuity of grace and merit, the issue being whether the *initium fidei,* the first motion of faith, comes from a human being's own turning to God, on his or her own power, or only through the power of God's grace and motion. This was decided by the Church in the second Council of Orange in 529, but this council was not known from before Aquinas's period right up into the sixteenth century. Moreover, the issue itself was not known either. But Aquinas discovered it in the later portion of his life, presumably through reading the later works of Augustine where he discussed the semi-Pelagian issue, but without using that term. Aquinas then clearly assumed Augustine's position. Cf. Bouillard, pp. 92–122.

25. Ibid., p. 151.

26. Cf. Otto H. Pesch, "Existential and Sapiential Theology—The Theological Confrontation between Luther and Thomas Aquinas," *Catholic Scholars Dialogue with Luther,* ed. Jared Wicks (Chicago: Loyola University Press, 1970), pp. 61–81.

27. Cf. M.-D. Chenu, *Toward Understanding Saint Thomas,* trans. Albert Landry and Dominic Hughes (Chicago: Henry Regnery Co., 1964), pp. 58–69.

28. Experience is not excluded by Aquinas. On the contrary, he asserts that God must move a person according to human nature and human nature is free and therefore conscious (*ST,* I–II, 113, 3). Moreover, later on in the *Summa,* in his treatment of the virtue of penance, Aquinas does give a description of conversion that is concrete and to a certain extent psychological. Conversion consists of turning toward

God, an act of faith, a movement of servile fear, a commitment to amendment and hope of pardon, a movement of charity and finally of filial fear of God (*ST,* III, 85, 5). This psychological analysis will reappear in the Council of Trent's *Decree on Justification.* This analysis of Aquinas, however, is less a subjective phenomenology and more an objective logical ordering of the acts involved in conversion (see *ST,* III, 85, 6). In whatever order these movements occur, it is the infusion of charity that constitutes the moment of justification.

29. Francis Colborn, "The Theology of Grace: Present Trends and Future Directions," *Theological Studies* 31 (1970): 711. It should be added here that if the interrelation between God and human beings is actual and real, then it must be able to be and ultimately should be rendered in ontological terms as well. What is needed, then, are ontological conceptions that are not inimical to phenomenological and descriptive accounts of personal experience and encounter. As will be seen in a later chapter, Karl Rahner has tried to open up the Roman Catholic ontological language of grace to this other level of discourse.

30. Eugene TeSelle, "The Problem of Nature and Grace," *The Journal of Religion* 45 (July 1965): 238–241.

31. It should be understood that we are dealing in this criticism with the formal concept of the supernatural and not the material supernature that would consist in the actual effects of grace. We are not calling into question the real effects of grace as presented in the section "Grace in Aquinas."

An example of an open concept of nature would be found in an infralapsarian view of the necessity of grace in which human nature of itself (Adamic nature) would be seen as "naturally" in a personal union with God were it not for sin. Grace would then be defined exclusively over against sin and not nature; it would *restore* nature to its natural state.

4
Luther: Sin and Grace

The reformation was both a reaction and an action. Highlighting the element of reaction, McNally writes: "The undeniably decadent state of the Church in the 15th century—especially its moral corruption, progressive secularization, decadent theology, irresponsible administration, and voluntaristic piety—cannot be overlooked as prime factors in bringing down the House of God and dispersing the faithful."[1] Highlighting the element of action, Chadwick recalls that the cause of the Reformation was not simply the corruption of the Church since that had existed for some time. The real reason was not that Europe was irreligious but that it was religious.[2] In approaching any reformer, then, one should try to keep in mind that what from a Roman Catholic point of view seems like a revolution is from a Protestant point of view a genuine reform. And this reform was sparked by authentic religious experience and motivation. The reformers gradually came to lose their belief in the fact that the de facto existing Church of the period was the real Church of Christ. Theirs was an effort to reestablish it.

In keeping with this broad polarity, the interpretation of Luther that follows will run along two basic themes. The first is the theme of comparison and contrast, which corresponds to the fundamental intentionality of this book. From such a contrast it will be seen that the reaction spawned basic differences in theological method and in the understanding of human existence, God, and our relationship with God in grace. These differences, moreover, reach very far into the understanding of Christian life and of Christianity itself. Secondly, there will be an effort of positive theological hermeneutics. Here it will be seen that on the most fundamental issues of grace and justification, Luther's positions have an internal consistency of their own that to a large extent are not contradictory relative to Roman Catholic understanding, but rather are simply different. And, finally, in all of this our reflections will be quite narrowly focused around Luther's earlier work, especially as it is represented in *The Freedom of the Christian.*

Historical Background

Without going into the enormous question of the state of the Church or the political situation of Europe immediately prior to the appearance of Luther, some specific incidents and conditions should be mentioned as symbolic of the period. They will help in the understanding of the man Luther and his theology.

First of all, when Tetzel arrived in a neighboring town preaching the papal plenary indulgence in 1517, Luther reacted and he did so out of spiritual motives. He was concerned with the Christian faith-life of the people. In the letter he sent to Albrecht of Mainz on October 31, 1517, accompanying his "Theses on Indulgences" and his "Treatise on Indulgences," he clearly states what these others reflect, that "his concern is stirred by the errors and misunderstandings that are spreading among the people."[3] That Tetzel's preaching of the indulgence was erroneous and spiritually harmful, that the official document promulgating and regulating the preaching of the indulgence contained "careless and exaggerated formulations,"[4] and that the whole theology of grace in connection with the practical use of relics and indulgences was ambiguous and confused—all of this makes up one element that is important, namely, what Luther was reacting against. But perhaps more important is the fact that Luther's motive for reacting is consistent with the whole thrust of his theology up until that time. A central theme in that theology is a pastoral concern for the Christian life, for Christian religious experience and the concrete living of it, in short, for Christian spirituality.[5]

In this light, one can better understand the continuities and differences that Luther's theology shares with Nominalism, that is, the theology antecedent to Luther and in which he was educated. A very basic theme that is common to both Nominalism and Luther is that of the absolute transcendence of God. In Nominalism, the emphasis on the transcendence of God, as seen in such theological categories as God's absolute power (*potentia absoluta*) as opposed to his ordered power (*potentia ordinata*), and the "divine acceptance," whereby "nothing has to be accepted by God," is a clear point of distinction between the old school (*via antiqua*) of Thomists, for example, and the new school (*via moderna*) of Nominalist Scholasticism. And whether this deeply religious insight was mediated to Luther by his early training in Nominalism or simply by the piety of the period, it remains one of the most fundamental qualities of his own religious experience and theology.[6]

Luther, however, is probably best typified by his attack against Nominalist Scholasticism. As early as 1516 and 1517 he was staging disputations against Scholastic theology through his students. The focus of this attack was the latent Pelagianism and semi-Pelagianism in the Nominalist concern for what human beings could do toward their salvation without God's grace.[7] The Nominalists had a generally optimistic view of human nature and its powers; it was not totally corrupted by the effects of original sin. In their conception, human beings retain their power to love God above all things *ex puris naturalibus.* And to the person who does all that is in his or her power, God will not deny his grace (*facienti quod in se est, Deus non denegat gratiam*).[8] To this optimism regarding human power before God, Luther's reaction was an absolute and unqualified no. At the core of all of Luther's assertions that surround his doctrine of justification and of faith and works, that is, his *sola fide,* his "through Christ," his *sola gratia,* is his adamant anti-Pelagianism.

Still another element in the Scholastic theology before Luther certainly has bearing on his own. The Nominalist tradition restricted both the sphere of and human confidence in what reason could determine about metaphysical reality and about God. Oberman writes that Nominalist epistemology was not intended to restrict knowledge of this world: "The purpose of this epistemology is rather to show the deficiencies in man's natural knowledge of *God*."[9] The Nominalist tradition, therefore, was extremely sceptical about the huge syntheses or *summas* of high Scholasticism, which reasoned so coherently about the superterrestrial order. And by contrast, this reverence concerning God's transcendence and mystery and this modesty concerning the human power to determine metaphysical truth actually enhanced the value of revelation. What was revealed and based on the divine authority of Scripture and the Church was accepted precisely as that, as revelation. The Nominalists insisted on a clear distinction between the sphere of reason and that of revelation and faith.[10] But by the same token this in turn narrowed down the field of revelation proper to what was explicitly taught and in so doing opened up whole areas of theology to the speculation of natural reason and logic.[11] And these logical speculations about what God could have done or what might be had little relation to religious experience and faith-life.

The charge that late Scholasticism was decadent becomes meaningful in the light of its being divorced from the experience, religious life and piety of the people. "These theologians are happy in their self love," wrote Desiderius Erasmus in 1509, "and as if they were presently inhabiting a third heaven, they look down on all men as though they were animals that crawled along the ground, coming near to pity them. They are protected by a wall of scholastic definitions, arguments, corollaries, and implicit and explicit propositions."[12] With the humanists, then, Luther reacted against this theology. Although he had nothing against reason if it remained in its place, he considered that the use Scholasticism made of reason distorted the data of faith and revelation, and that ultimately it threatened the doctrine of grace.[13] He fiercely resented Aquinas precisely because he blamed him for introducing Aristotle into Christian theology. And of Aristotle, Luther wrote: "This defunct pagan has attained supremacy; impeded, and almost suppressed, the Scriptures of the living God. When I think of this lamentable state of affairs, I cannot avoid believing that the Evil One introduced the study of Aristotle."[14] A biblical scholar and Doctor of Scripture himself, Luther's early attacks on Scholasticism coincided with his efforts at a gradual biblical renewal of theology at Wittenberg in the period immediately preceding the indulgence controversy. And the logic of this is quite consistent: If Church and theology are in a state of corruption and in need of reform, it is natural to look back at origins, at revelation as it appears in Scripture and at the early work of the Fathers in order to find some sort of norm and criterion for the reformation. Theologically, Luther's reform was through a movement back to the sources.

Luther's Religious Experience
It is often insisted that Luther's theology is very intimately con-

nected with his own religious experience. Ultimately, a full understanding in the sense of an explanation of his or any theology must in one way or another be led back to religious experience as an essential element of the genesis and origin of ideas.[15]

Experience

Luther's life as an Augustinian monk began in 1505, and as it turned out it was not an altogether spiritually peaceful one. On the one hand, he had a deep sense of his own sin and on the other he tended to look upon God as an implacable judge. As a monk, he led a very ascetic life of fasting and prayer, vigils and choir, but it brought him little spiritual equilibrium. He was scrupulous and wondered if all of his sins were confessed. Ultimately his frequent and for some periods daily confession did not bring him into a peaceful relationship with God. Although he was encouraged by his spiritual director, Johann von Staupitz, at Wittenberg, his difficulties continued. Eventually he came to realize that something is more drastically wrong with human existence than the offenses that can be enumerated, confessed and forgiven. The very "nature" of humanity is sinful. Urged to simply love God, Luther frequently fell back in desolation, separation and alienation from God approaching despair. He later wrote:

> Is it not against all natural reason that God out of his mere whim deserts men, hardens them, damns them, as if he delighted in sins and in such torments of the wretched for eternity, he who is said to be of such mercy and goodness? This appears iniquitous, cruel, and intolerable in God, by which very many have been offended in all ages. And who would not be? I was myself more than once driven to the very abyss of despair so that I wished I had never been created. Love God? I hated him![16]

Structure of Experience

There is no need to go into a psychological analysis of Luther's personality to explain his religious experience. Such origins, whether they were psychological or from the medieval period itself in which Luther lived, have very little to do with value. However, a certain structure in Luther's experience does emerge, a structure having more than purely personal relevance. Luther's was a kind of primitive religious experience that can be awakened in any person should he or she dwell on the fact that God is God and that we are what we are.[17]

This structure may be characterized as a sense and fear of the Infinite and Holy and a corresponding sense of unworthiness. In this structure God appears as the *mysterium tremendum*, the awful and terrifying God of power and might.[18] God is experienced as absolutely transcendent: He is infinitude, he is the Almighty. God's majesty and glory blind the lowly creature. He is all holy and no unholiness can stand in his presence; he smites impurity with his justice, his anger and his wrath. Before such a God, human persons can feel only their own weakness, their smallness as creatures and their sinfulness as human beings. Standing before the infinite and all-holy God, people cannot conceive of themselves as being good; they are precisely impure and self-willed sinners.

The Experience of Forgiveness

There can be no doubt of the fact that Luther did reach a stage or some degree of spiritual peace and stability during his life. And without going into the details of how this religious experience developed, for that is not the point here, it can be said that his later religious experience also had a structure. That structure can be seen in a paradox. It consists in perceiving, in the moments of greatest spiritual torment, the loving God behind the holy and commanding God. It grasps above and beyond the fear inspired by the infinite justice and wrath of God the mystery of infinite love manifested in God's promise of mercy and the saving work of Christ. It hears within the no of God's condemnation of human sin God's benevolent yes of acceptance and forgiveness. And paradoxically, only when one feels most unworthy and when one's last claim on salvation has disappeared, when nothing remains but a readiness to surrender to God's almighty will and judgment, only then can one feel that God accepts and forgives a person as he or she actually is.

The structure of this experience of God is such that the two moments of the paradox are simultaneous. Human beings remain creature, empty and unworthy, and in their sin they abandon themselves to God's mercy. And God's mercy attains its full dimension precisely to the extent that we realize that we are accepted in our unworthiness. Only when human existence is emptied in itself is it in that same moment and to that same degree filled with the fullness of God's grace.[19]

Theology

In answering the question of how this new experience of God came about, or of the source of what can be seen as a resolution of Luther's spiritual struggles, one has to point to his work as a biblical theologian. He began lecturing on the Psalms in 1513, on Romans in 1515 and on Galatians in 1516. Moreover, he read Augustine's anti-Pelagian work, especially his *De Spiritu et Littera*, during this period. And Paul and Augustine appear as two of the major influences on his theology. For this reason, the years beginning with 1513 have usually been considered extremely important in the shaping of Luther's thought. And the "Tower Experience," referring to where he studied and prepared his lectures on Scripture during these years, is often considered to mark an important development in his spiritual progress and in his theology.

Again, one does not have to trace specific events in that development to see that there is a close interaction and correlation between Luther's own personal religious experience and the forming of that experience through the study of Scripture and the Fathers. On the one hand, Luther was trying to understand God and himself in the light of his faith. And gradually Scripture became the dominant force that shaped what he knew of God and of himself. Later on he would point to Scripture as the one supreme authority that can ultimately determine Christian consciousness. On the other hand, dialectically, Luther's inner religious experience was interpreting Scripture. In studying Scripture, the earliest record of the first faith of Christians and of the determining events of Christian revelation, Luther had to bring to bear his own inner experience. Experience alone allows one to discern one's sources, so it is not surprising that Luther's understanding of Christianity owes so much to the light and force of his own religious experience.

Luther's *theology*, that is, his *understanding* of God and human existence in the light of Christian faith and its sources, emerges therefore with a peculiarly vital and experiential quality to it. It is a theology that is ultimately connected with religious faith-life and with pastoral concern. It is a theology that carries a personal religious conviction that recalls Augustine. And, finally, as far as content is concerned, in the course of this evolution, the concept of faith and the forgiveness of sin gradually assumed a central place in his understanding of grace and justification and the Christian life.

The Theology of Luther

It is far beyond the scope of this chapter to give a detailed critical analysis of Luther's theology. What follow are simply general characteristics of his mode of doing theology that, when placed in contrast with the theology of Aquinas, allow one to see how different are these theological worlds.

As a very first qualification, it may be noted that Luther was not a systematic theologian. His writings cover a long period of time in which there were developments. His positions, moreover, unfold in a variety of literary genres—commentaries on Scripture and polemical tracts, theses for disputation, treatises for instruction and sermons, letters, pamphlets and technical monographs. One cannot give a systematic account of Luther's theology, and all reductions of his theology of sin and grace to a series of abstract propositions or formulae are necessarily inadequate.[20] At best, one can only locate certain centers of his thought, basic ideas or themes or organic principles, around which other ideas gravitate, interrelate and become bound together. One such idea would be "forgiveness of sins" which is so intimately connected with justification by faith.[21] Beyond this one could also say that Luther was a biblical theologian, especially influenced by Paul and Augustine in his doctrines of sin and grace, and that the idea of justification by faith is also very close to the center of his theology.

Definition of Theology

A striking difference between Aquinas and Luther is seen in their definitions of what theology is. Introducing his *Summa Theologiae*, Aquinas defined theology in the following way:

Christian theology should be pronounced to be a science. Yet bear in mind that sciences are of two kinds: some work from premises recognized in the innate light of intelligence, . . . while others work from premises recognized in the light of a higher science. . . . In this second manner is Christian theology a science, namely God's very own which he shares with the blessed.[22]

Luther in turn offers the following as one definition of theology:

The proper subject of theology is man guilty of sin and condemned, and God the Justifier and Savior of man the sinner. Whatever is asked or discussed in theology outside this subject, is error and poison.[23]

Mode of Theological Thinking

Otto Pesch contrasts the different ways of doing theology, the different kinds of theological thinking, that these two definitions represent. He labels Aquinas's "Sapiential Theology" and Luther's "Existential Theology."

In Aquinas, theology is a science in the medieval sense of understanding a matter through its ultimate ontological causes. As the definition shows and as his understanding of human-being-in-grace reveals, this science is analogous to Aristotelian science although its first principles come from a different source. In Luther, however, theology is not an attempt at "science," that is, an organized explanation of one's relation to God through objective metaphysical causes. It aims simply at an understanding of oneself and of human existence as it stands before God. In Aquinas faith is the basis of theological statements, but in the sense that one accepts the sources of revelation as an authority and works from there. The articles of the creed act as first principles. In Luther, actual faith experience finds its way into all of his statements. Theology is speaking out of faith experience so that the act of faith is active in theologizing itself. In Aquinas, theology has an objective quality; it describes reality, as it were, "out-there," and is less a form of confessional statement. In Luther theology tends to be precisely confessional. Whereas Aquinas speaks theologically of God in the third person, in the I-It context of an "object" to be studied, Luther speaks of God in more experiential terms, that is, in the I-Thou context of personal relation and encounter. Pesch sums up the differences of these two modes of theology in the following way:

> By way of definition we might say the following. *Sapiential theology* is the way of doing theology from outside one's self-actuation in the existence in faith, in the sense that in its doctrinal statements the faith and confession of the speaker is the enduring presupposition, but is not thematic within this theology. This theology strives to mirror and recapitulate God's own thoughts about the world, men, and history, insofar as God has disclosed them. *Existential theology* is the way of doing theology from within the self-actuation of our existence in faith, as we submit to God in the obedience of faith. Its affirmations are so formulated that the actual faith and confession of the speaker are not merely necessary presuppositions but are reflexly thematized.[24]

Framework for Understanding Grace

Whereas the data concerning God's grace comes from revelation, from Scripture, the creed and the Fathers, Aquinas's framework for understanding it is scientific in terms of Greek philosophy. The whole economy of redemption is seen in the context of God and his creation; his treatise on grace fits into the Neoplatonic scheme of creation returning to its creator, but on a supernatural level. The categories Aquinas uses in his theology are taken from Aristotle's physics and metaphysics. The basic problematic to which grace responds is that of nature, both in the sense of "creation" and "human nature." This means that we need grace not primarily because of our sin, but more fundamentally because we are creatures and the end to which we are called and toward which we must move through our activity absolutely transcends the teleological capabilities of our created nature. And, finally, the reality itself of grace is being and therefore can be analyzed according to the categories of being as a quality and habit inhering in the soul. Grace is a qualitative disposition in the soul that is equivalently a new nature raising up human existence and actions to a level proportionate to the end to which it is called.

By contrast, Luther's main concern with grace centers on human sinfulness. This too is a concern for salvation but the obstacle to that salvation is sin; the fundamental problematic to which grace responds and the context in which it is understood is therefore moral in the sense of concerning human worth or value. It is the context of the personal relationship with God, or the interpersonal context of the human person standing before the living God. Only derivatively and secondarily does grace concern human responsibility and the quality of human freedom, behavior and action. In the first place grace responds to the worth of human existence in the eyes of the living God and this is most fundamentally viewed in terms of sinfulness. The language and categories used will therefore be those defined by such a context, namely, the categories of personal relationships as these are seen in Scripture.

It should be noted that these differences are real and very fundamental. Moreover, as long as one stays on this very broad level, they can to some extent be generalized into basically different understandings of grace among Catholics and Portestants. Until recently and in a sense even now, for the Catholic grace is a new elevating nature that raises up and sanctifies. Added to nature, it raises a person up to be a son of God, where "son of God" takes on a precise meaning of a new divine nature and life, a new level of being. For the Protestant, grace is not a response to nature at all, at least not in a metaphysical sense, but to human sinfulness. It does not add to human nature; if anything it helps to restore it. In the words of TeSelle: "It is usual in Protestant theology to speak of grace as the free and unmerited activity of God for the benefit of the sinner, overcoming his bondage to sin and restoring him to the life for which he was originally destined." This may be opposed to a peculiarly Catholic tradition that "has insisted that grace is not exhausted by its function of overcoming sin. God is gracious not only to man as sinner but also to man *as man*. Even apart from sin it is proper to speak of grace, in that man is brought into a relationship with God which is not an inherent possibility of man himself but is only made possible by God's self communication."[25]

Luther's Doctrine of Grace

This brief sketch of Luther's doctrine of sin, grace and justification is dictated by the very narrowly focused intention mentioned at the outset. It means to present only certain key themes, especially those that appear in *The Freedom of the Christian*, and in which the differences in the language of Luther and Aquinas are highlighted. The consistency of Luther's own language of grace will thus appear all the more striking. Four such central themes can be discerned.

Simul Justus et Peccator

In his lectures on Romans (1515–1516) Luther already identified sin and concupiscence. He wrote: "Therefore actual sin (as the theologians call it) is, strictly speaking, the work and fruit of sin, and sin itself is that passion (tinder) and concupiscence, or that inclination toward evil and resistance against the good. . . . "[26] Because concupiscence remains after faith and justification, a person remains a sinner even in his or her acceptance of God's work of pardon and forgiveness; saints are precisely those who confess their sinfulness before God. But at the same time, conversion involves a radical change and metanoia in the human person because sin was unchecked before faith. In Luther's early writings the recognition of sinfulness and the change in one's self-evaluation, together with accepting forgiveness from God alone, formed the elements of a dialectic that made faith-life a constant process or movement toward an extinction of sin. But this would not, of course, come about in this world.

In his dealing with the question of sin and grace, Luther thinks of a human being's situation before God in personal categories and in terms of relations. In a person's relationship with God, sin and grace are not exclusive or contradictory terms. Grace is the relation of friendship and communion established by God *in spite* of a person's sinfulness, that is, the basic unworthiness that is manifested in concupiscence and that remains. There is no metaphysical absurdity in saying that a person remains unworthy and yet is accepted. In fact, it corresponds to our experience of the actual state of the case. Thus Pesch says:

Here we have reached the ultimate cause of Luther's *simul*. It has been well described as "a reality of prayer." The sin that remains after justification emerges in one's own prayerful self-description before God, and only there. This means that the *simul peccator* occurs as one formulates his own existence in faith, where at the same time he is prayerfully accepting God's word of grace. The more theoretical and dogmatic formulation of the *simul justus et peccator* is nothing more than a subsequent descriptive statement of an affirmation originating within an I-thou encounter with God. Thus Luther's *simul* is a classic example of existential theology, i.e., of the theology which seeks to make thematic our very existence in faith.[27]

By contrast, in Aquinas's language, which is modeled on Aristotle's conception of the generation of a substance, sin and grace are exclusive realities. When Aquinas deals with the successive phases of justification, it appears that justification is instantaneous; the moment justifying grace takes hold of the soul it is at that instant *not* in sin.[28] This is so because he is thinking in the ontological categories of habits and qualities according to the model of being or not being a certain kind of reality. In this language it is metaphysically absurd that a person be in sin and grace at the same time—water cannot be hot and cold at the same time. Sin and grace are contrary states ontologically; logically they are contradictory; they are mutually exclusive. On this quesion, the language of Aquinas, the Scholastics and Trent does not communicate with Luther. It is simply different.

Justification

In his lectures on Romans and Galatians the themes of the forgiveness of sins and God's nonimputation of the evil that is in man begin to emerge with more and more clarity. Gradually the *essence* of justification came to be seen by Luther as *forgiveness of sin*. In terms of Law and Gospel, that is, the two words of God, commandments and promises, one is justified when he or she receives the word of God's mercy, benevolence and forgiveness. Grace is God's word of forgiveness.[29] Because people remain sinners and unworthy, their righteousness is imputed: "So Paul says in Rom. 4 [:3] that Abraham's faith 'was reckoned to him as righteousness' because by it he gave glory most perfectly to God, and that for the same reason our faith shall be reckoned to us as righteousness if we believe."[30]

Because of this core of "the forgiveness of sin," imputed justice or reckoned righteousness, Luther's doctrine of justification often became characterized by Catholics as "mere imputation." In the sharp realism of Scholastic language, grace is conceived of as a created mode of being in the soul, a habit and new nature that effected a new way of being of the soul and consequently of the human person. Because in Luther the person remains a sinner, it was thought that for him grace had no created effect in human "being" or existence. And on his part, Luther simply denied the Scholastic conception of grace: "Grace must be properly understood as the 'favor of God', not as a 'quality of soul.' "[31] In effect, then, the Scholastic mind tended to regard "mere imputed justice" as no justification at all.

Whereas the essence of justification is real forgiveness of sin, and paradoxically Luther could insist on this, it is also much more than this. Thus the interpretation of Luther's doctrine of justification as "mere imputed justice" is simply erroneous. Although Luther thinks in terms of relationships, one's relationships with Christ effects a *radical* and *real* change in the human person, one that is often expressed in striking images. "Just as the heated iron glows like fire because of the union of fire with it, so the Word imparts its qualities to the soul."[32] Although it is not described in Greek metaphysical and ontological categories, the union of a person with Christ is real and for this reason the image of Christ as bridegroom developed in *Freedom* is extremely important.[33] And, finally, the sanctifying action of the Holy Spirit within the person is intimately related to justification. Shortly before *Freedom* Luther wrote:

> Given this faith, there immediately follows the most precious affection of the heart, enlarging and deepening the human soul, i.e., love as given by the Holy Spirit through faith in Christ. Thus the believer draws near to Christ, that loving and bounteous testator, and becomes a new and different man through and through.[34]

Faith Alone (Grace Alone)

The statement that justification is through faith alone has an almost absolute quality in Luther's theology. It is a statement that is equivalent to "by grace alone" and to "through Christ alone." It must be understood in the context of Luther's absolute anti-Pelagianism. Luther asserts that a person's salvation is effected in utter and absolute gratuity and through the work of another, Christ.[35] Faith, then, is not a work or a self-initiated act; it is a self-surrender and pure reception that renounces all efforts of self-justification. In terms of the faith-works contrast, no external works or religious observances justify, for justification is effected in the inner spiritual arena through faith. Works are considered by Luther as simply external acts in an exclusive sense.

> For the person is justified and saved, not by works or laws, but by the Word of God, that is, by the promise of his grace, and by faith, that the glory may remain God's who saved us not by works of righteousness which we have done, but by virtue of his mercy by the word of his grace when we believed.[36]

Faith gradually assumed more and more importance in Luther's theology. It is not an intellectual assent, as in Scholasticism, but an infinitely more complex attitude toward and relationship with God. But the most important of all its elements is its existential quality. What James says of prayer, that it is religion in act, applies to Luther on faith. Faith is the existential actuality of the human person in relation with God. That faith is the very ground and basis of Christian life and the prerequisite of grace is traditional Christian doctrine. But when Luther highlighted its necessarily personal and existential aspect, and even its psychologically actual dimension, as his whole theology tended to do, it resulted in a view of things very different from that which Scholastic language allows.

Aquinas and Trent both say that a certitude about grace and salvation is impossible. In Aquinas, the matter is viewed from the outside, from outside one's concrete and actual faith experience. From this point of view God's fidelity to our salvation is certain; but in view of human weakness and instability, since a person can at any moment reject God's grace, one cannot affirm certitude of final salvation. In Luther, however, the question is answered from within the act of faith itself. From this point of view, the distinction between God and the human person as objectively described cannot be made. Faith *is* the certainty of the trust in God's gift and fidelity. To speak of uncertainty in faith is to cancel the very act of faith. The certainty that Luther is talking about is not a category of knowledge, that is, certain knowledge, as it is in the Thomistic discussion. Rather it is a way of existing. Quite simply, then, when Trent and Luther said no and yes rspectively to the question of certainty of grace and salvation, they were not responding to the same question.[37]

Cooperation and Merit

Aquinas approaches the question of cooperation with grace and consequently merit from his metaphysical and scientific point of view. Grace is first of all a new nature infused in the soul that justifies. This new nature is also a principle of activity and hence a second effect of grace is meritorious activity. Three reasons underlie Aquinas's affirmation of merit: He must preserve human freedom; a person does not remain lifeless under God's grace nor does God manipulate people.[38] Second, he wants to protect God's justice, God's dealing with right and wrong conduct in the whole moral order.[39] And, finally, the whole Neoplatonic and Augustinian framework into which his treatise on grace fits is one that sees human existence, coming from God, now on its way *back* toward God, to whom all things are ordained teleologically as to their end, but now on a new supernatural level. God's grace thus works through human freedom into personal actions that are salvific, moving a person toward salvation. In all of this, however, Aquinas is of course thoroughly anti-Pelagian; grace is always prior.[40]

By contrast, grace in Luther is fundamentally a relationship; grace is God's favor. And in his response to Erasmus, the *De Servo Arbitrio* of 1525, Luther states categorically that there is no such thing as merit. But his denial is not asserted on the basis of a structural analysis of the relation between divine and human force producing a good act as in Aquinas's discussion of cooperative grace. For him the gratuity of grace, based on our total undeservedness over against God's total benevolence toward us, the fact that we remain sinners *coram Deo*, excludes the very idea of achieving or meriting salvation with any power of our own whatsoever. In the words of Brian Gerrish:

Luther found it irrelevant to ask *how* a man *can* acquire merit (be it by his own native efforts or by an infusion of divine grace).

He considered grace and merit to be mutually exclusive; and on this view the mere claim *that* men *must* acquire merit, or else remain unsaved, has already translated them out of the realm of grace (if by "grace" we mean God's unmerited favour) into the realm of legal requirements, grace being preserved only in name.[41]

It is right at this point that one can see how these two conceptions of grace, these different languages, can generate two very different spiritualities, two different understandings of the Christian life, each with practical consequences and each with its inherent dangers.[42] The Catholic conception has the merit of preserving human freedom even while asserting God's grace, and of seeing our relation with God being played out in the sacramental life and our concrete behavior in this world. But it has an inherent danger of legalism in the sense that salvation is won by a person after his or her conversion; it is a reward of the Christian life. Underlying this view are Greek philosophical categories of moving toward an end that human existence and hence a person *desires*, that is, one's own happiness and blessedness. There is a tendency to see the Christian as attaining this goal by performing activities and to see discrete acts of virtue as increasing a merit proportionate to that goal. There can be no doubt that even though all this can be asserted in grace and only because of grace, there is still a danger of legalism, that is, gaining salvation through ritual and moral behavior.[43]

Luther's spirituality has the advantage of its total anti-Pelagianism. Our ability to earn salvation, our radical dependence on grace, is affirmed not only *before* but also *after* justification. God's acceptance of a person is radically distinguished from his or her ethical and moral behavior. And as will be seen below, Luther's conception of the Christian life is supremely altruistic: By justification through faith the Christian is freed to serve the neighbor without an eye for self-sanctification.[44] However, by the same token, Luther's view of the human person seems to be demeaning. Moreover there is a tendency toward a dualism and separation between the two kingdoms and the inner and outer spheres of human existence. And because of this there is a danger of not integrating people's external and this-worldly behavior into their religious faith-life. A result could be a failure to see that there is an intimate connection between external behavior and the inner person; one *is* what one *does*. Such a dualism would not see people working out their graced existence in their concrete human life in this world, both in sacramental life and in concrete ethical and moral life.[45]

Contributions to a Theology of Grace

There are any number of very basic ideas that Luther contributes to the theology of grace. But besides the theme of the forgiveness of sins, three other notions might be underlined because they seem to confirm essential elements in the Christian experience of grace and its understanding, and because they have special relevance for today.

Being Raised Up

Today more and more Catholic theologians are abandoning the Scholastic language of grace, both because it is not a common language and because of its inherent limitations. They are calling for a theology of grace in personalist categories. Scholastic theology, however, expresses the elevating quality of grace in an extremely clear way and shows the reality of the transformation that occurs in human existence under God's grace. What is needed is a way to express this in personalist categories with equal force and clarity. Luther and Lutheran tradition help in this regard.

In his bridal image, Luther conceives of the human person's union with Christ as a bride to her bridegroom. The relation is between two persons, an intimate union where the two become one because of the love bestowed on the beloved. What is important here is to see the transfer of qualities in this interpersonal relationship. Christ takes upon himself a person's weakness and debility through this interpersonal bond, and the beloved, precisely by the uniting bond of love, is raised up to Christ's level.

> Here this rich and divine bridegroom Christ marries this poor, wicked harlot, redeems her from all her evil, and adorns her with all his goodness. Her sins cannot now destroy her, since they are laid upon Christ and swallowed up by him. And she

has that righteousness in Christ, her husband, of which she may boast as of her own and which she can confidently display alongside her sins in the face of death and hell.[46]

The point here, namely that love has the power of making lovers equal, can be illustrated by a parable adapted from Soren Kierkegaard.[47] Once there was a great king and a poor servant girl, and the young king fell in love with the humble maiden. They were to be married. However, by every human standard it could not possibly work: The servant girl was obviously below the station and class of the king and his family. The equality that is absolutely necessary for real or authentic love to obtain would certainly be lacking. The girl must feel inferior, crushed and in despair, and protestation on the part of the lover king would only worsen matters, for it would be taken as pity. And pity is not love. But by a paradox of love it would work, even though it could not, if the king really loved the girl. For the very fact of his love would raise her up and bestow on her a value and worth that would make her his equal. And paradoxically, for this to happen, she need simply remain herself, trusting that after all the king must know what he is about in loving her as she is. This creative power of love is not rational or logical. It works rather by a logic of its own.

In another context, Tillich describes the power and force of what is going on here in terms of "creative justice." Creative justice is an interpersonal relation that works through or is actuated by love. Its qualities are "listening," "giving" and "forgiving." And when this is applied to the relationship of God with the human person, one has the power of justification in which God accepts and bestows divine worth on human existence. What is most important in Tillich's presentation of creative justice, however, is the fact that it is a question of ontology and being. This is not a question of "mere" psychology. Although expressed in personalist categories and in terms of relations, what occurs in this relationship has the power of being within it; it is a question of ontology and of really being raised up.[48]

Freedom from the World

The second theme from Luther's theology of grace that bears emphasis is that grace and the union with God that it effects raises human existence up above the world and frees it from the world. Luther explains this in the context of his image of marriage with Christ in which the believer shares in Christ's kingship. Through union with Christ, "every Christian is by faith so exalted above all things that, by virtue of a spiritual power, he is lord of all things without exception, so that nothing can do him any harm."[49] Luther goes on to explain that this does not mean that one has the power of physical control in the world; it is a spiritual power and dominion and an inner freedom that liberates one from every power in this world.

A development of this idea reappears in the theology of Tillich as the "Protestant principle." The Protestant principle rejects the claim of every finite and relative thing in this world to absoluteness, to taking the place of God, to our absolute commitment or allegiance.[50] Tillich himself tells how this principle is derived from the Pauline-Lutheran interpretation of justification, which denies every human claim before God.[51] But this theme of God's transcendence and human participation in it and consequent freedom and liberation through his grace cannot be limited to Lutheranism; it seems rather to be one of the central effects of the religious experience of God's grace. In God's word of forgiveness, mercy and love, and in one's union with him, human beings are freed from themselves, from the world and from the very judgment of God himself. This allows the Christian to overcome all fear and it relativizes everything finite, every cultural product and every institution. All is finite precisely in relation to God, and may be challenged as such. This effect of grace plays a large role in contemporary theologies of hope, of history and of liberation. It is difficult to see how any Christian church will play a major role in the liberation of other human beings without this "freedom from the world and from fear" in Christ.

Freedom for the Neighbor

Third, the extremely idealistic and peculiarly Christian notion of freedom for the neighbor that appears as the fruit of grace in Luther's theology must be underlined. The freedom from sin and self that God's grace, justification and salvation effects within people need in no way be escapist or quietist. "A man does not live for himself alone in this mortal body to work for it alone, but he lives also for all men on earth; rather, he lives only for others and not for himself."[52]

Luther's reason for asserting this freedom is quite separate from any philosophical notion of teleology, of human existence moving toward its end or goal, happiness in God, and from every idea of using creation and activity in this world as a means to this end. In Augustine and Aquinas *caritas* tends to mean love of God and of the neighbor for God's sake. In Luther *caritas* usually means love of neighbor for his or her own sake.[53] In Luther the Christian is already justified and saved through faith and thus is free, freed to serve the neighbor for his or her own sake. Because of what has been done to him, the Christian

> may serve and benefit others in all that he does, considering nothing except the need and the advantage of his neighbor. . . . Here faith is truly active through love, that is, it finds its expression in works of the freest service, cheerfully and lovingly done, with which a man willingly serves another without hope of reward; and for himself he is satisfied with the fullness and wealth of his faith.[54]

Here Luther appears strikingly optimistic, and his Christian idealism is in stark contrast to his conception of the human person as the self-willed sinner. No doubt such an ideal will be fulfilled only in the life of one person, Jesus, whom Bonhoeffer called "the man for others." But this is the ideal to which God's grace calls the Christian. Bonhoeffer even suggests that "this concern of Jesus for others [is] the experience of transcendence."[55]

Conclusion

Luther's language concerning grace is considerably different from that of Scholasticism and hence of Roman Catholicism. And precisely because each specific language has its own genius, it is able to illuminate specific and different aspects of reality. But for that very reason, languages must be set up as normative only with the most extreme caution and consideration. And to the extent that Luther's language is exclusive it can be criticized. Three difficulties or questions can be proposed.

In treating Augustine and his view of predestination, it was indicated that his view of human existence was too pessimistic. The same can be said of Luther. His view of human existence and of nature seems too negative. In fact, at one point Luther seems to have gone to the extreme of even denying human freedom and the possibility of self-determination. He seems to assert a deterministic universe predetermined by God's foreknowledge and immutable will.[56] But more generally, he tends to emphasize grace as so completely the work of God in us that he reduces almost to a vanishing point our free response. It must be seen that God's grace is all the more powerful and wonderful because it effects a completely free response of love on the part of a person to God.

Second, and closely related to the first problem, is the fact that Luther's theology of grace seems too closely aligned with his own faith experience. As a result, his language of grace is too conditioned by his "sick-souled" religious experience. Is there not more to grace than the moral context for forgiveness of sin and acceptance of the sinner allow to appear? "Is not God at work to communicate a new life, a new heart that can love [as is Augustine], a spirit honoring him in praise and adoration?"[57] These themes do appear in Luther, as has been shown, but they are obscured by too narrow a focus on human experience in its sin and its need for forgiveness. Luther's view of Christ and Christianity seems to appeal only to the weak and not to the strong. The doctrine of *simul justus et peccator* and the paradox of the two words of God—Law and Gospel—define a conception of grace whose contours are too constricting. There may be many other and more positive experiences of God's grace, "healthy-mindedness" being only one at the opposite extreme, which Luther's language of grace does not include. And as Avery Dulles has remarked: "Few of our contemporaries are so oppressed by the sense of guilt and depravity that they feel the imminent threat of eternal damnation."[58]

Finally, Luther's evangelical understanding of grace, like that of others of his period and before him, is too closely tied to explicit knowledge of Christianity. Practically speaking, Luther sees God's grace in the word of God that appears in the message of the Gospel that is preached and accepted in explicit faith.[59] But if God's salvific will is universal, it becomes difficult to limit God's grace to human existence by seeing it mediated only through the channel of an explicit knowledge or presentation of God's word of forgiveness as it appears in Jesus and Scripture. And if God's grace is operative through all of history and is effecting salvation there, it will be difficult to explain this in terms of the explicit Christian word of God received in faith. It seems almost necessary that one be thrown back into some sort of ontological categories to understand how God can be there, present and operating, without people's being explicitly aware of it through any direct contact with Christian Scripture and teaching. And it seems likely that this saving operation of God's grace outside explicit Christian awareness may well be mediated through a person's moral life, which the radical distinction between faith and works in Luther does not seem to permit. From this point of view, then, Luther's language of grace as it appears in his writings needs to be further developed.

Notes

1. Robert McNally, *The Reform of the Church* (New York: Sheed and Ward, 1963), p. 105.

2. Owen Chadwick, *The Reformation* (Baltimore: Penguin Books, 1964), p. 22.

3. Jared Wicks, *Man Yearning for Grace* (Washington, D.C.: Corpus Books, 1968), p. 227.

4. Ibid., p. 231.

5. This is a fundamental supposition and thesis in Wick's work *Man Yearning for Grace*.

6. For some other elements in Luther's thought that may have been inherited from Ockamist theology, cf. B. A. Gerrish, *Grace and Reason* (Oxford: Clarendon Press, 1962), pp. 43–56.

7. It should be recalled that the second Council of Orange (529) was not known during this period and so there is no question of formal heresy. Moreover, there were certain elements in the Nominalist system that mitigate the Pelagian tendency, viz., their emphasis on God's transcendence, his *potentia absoluta* and the *divina acceptatio*, the axiom *nil creatum acceptandum* (nothing created has to be accepted by God). In spite of this, however,

God is envisaged as having freely bound himself to the historical order of things and the description of how human beings could work out their salvation in this *de facto* order is generally considered in varying degrees both Pelagian and semi-Pelagian. Cf. Heiko A. Oberman, *The Harvest of Medieval Theology* (Cambridge, Mass.: Harvard University Press, 1963), pp. 177, 426.

8. Oberman, *The Harvest of Medieval Theology*, pp. 132, 175–177, 184.

9. Ibid., p. 41.

10. Ibid., pp. 56–57, 88.

11. Ibid., p. 51.

12. Desiderius Erasmus, *In Praise of Folly*, in *The Essential Erasmus*, ed. and trans. John P. Dolan (New York: Mentor Book, New American Library, 1964), p. 143.

13. Gerrish, *Grace and Reason,* pp. 136–137, 168–170.

14. Luther, "An Appeal to the Ruling Class of German Nationality as to the Amelioration of the State of Christendom," in *Martin Luther: Selections from His Writings*, ed. John Dillenberger (Garden City, N.Y.: Anchor Books, Doubleday & Co., 1961), pp. 470–471.

15. Wicks strongly cautions against relying too heavily on Luther's later autobiographical accounts of his religious experience as a basis for interpreting his early theology. It is not a reliable principle of interpretation and it has led in fact to many misinterpretations (Wicks, *Man Yearning for Grace*, pp. 9–10, 12, 265–268). The brief characterization of Luther's personal religious experience presented here, however, is not meant as a principle of interpretation from which definite or specific conclusion can be drawn as to his development. It is meant rather to help explain *why* he said what he said. Without some correlation to experience, no matter what tradition a theologian is located in or what the determined source from which he borrowed, one has still not explained why he borrowed from this tradition or that theologian and not another, why he focused on this text of Scripture and not another.

16. Cited from Roland Bainton, *Here I Stand: A Life of Martin Luther* (New York: Abingdon Press, 1950), p. 59.

17. Gerhard Ritter, *Luther: His Life and Works*, trans. John Riches (New York: Harper & Row, 1963), pp. 32–34; Bainton, *Here I Stand*, pp. 41–42.

18. The term *mysterium tremendum* is borrowed from Rudolf Otto's *The Idea of the Holy* (New York: A Galaxy Book, Oxford University Press, 1958) where this experience of God is analyzed phenomenologically and at length. In another mode, namely that of description, psychological typology and classification, there is no doubt that Luther shares qualities of William James's "sick-souled" religious experience. See James, *The Varieties of Religious Experience* (New York: Collier Books, 1961), pp. 114–142.

19. Cf. Bainton, *Here I Stand*, pp. 60–66. In describing this experience

we are more interested in its basic paradoxical structure than in its details. It is not suggested here that this characterization represents any full account of Luther's religious experience. And Wicks's study of Luther's early theology leads one to assert that this structure still did not dominate his spiritual theology during his early period, that is, up to 1518.

20. Jared Wicks, "Luther's Vision of Man in Sin and Grace," (Unpublished monograph, January 1970), p. 10.

21. Gerrish suggests two such central ideas: "In particular recent Luther-research has stressed the manner in which the entire structure of the Reformer's theology is determined by the doctrines of the 'two kingdoms' and of the forgiveness of sins. It is these two fundamental conceptions which give Luther's thinking such inner harmony as it has . . . " (*Grace and Reason*, p. 8).

22. Aquinas, *Summa Theologiae*, I, 1, 2.

23. Both of these definitions are cited from Otto Pesch, "Existential and Sapiential Theology—The Theological Confrontation between Luther and Thomas Aquinas," *Catholic Scholars Dialogue with Luther*, ed. Jared Wicks (Chicago: Loyola University Press, 1970), pp. 64–65. The contrast between Luther and Aquinas offered here is dependent on this work of Pesch.

24. Ibid., pp. 76–77. The order of the two definitions has been reversed.

25. Eugene TeSelle, "The Problem of Nature and Grace," *The Journal of Religion* 45 (July 1965): 238.

26. Luther, *Lectures on Romans*, cited from Wicks, "Vision," p. 13.

27. Pesch, "Existential and Sapiential Theology," p. 73.

28. *Summa Theologiae*, I–II, 113, 7. See also 113, 2.

29. Luther, *The Freedom of the Christian Man*, in Dillenberger, *Martin Luther*, pp. 53–58.

30. Luther, *Freedom*, p. 60.

31. Quoted from Gerrish, *Grace and Reason*, p. 129.

32. Luther, *Freedom*, p. 58.

33. Ibid., pp. 60–61.

34. Luther, *The Pagan Servitude of the Church*, in Dillenberger, *Martin Luther*, p. 275. Grace and justification are still thought of as essentially forgiveness and it is here that one sees the difference between Luther and Augustine. Basically, the problems that Augustine and Luther were addressing were different. In both the Law condemns. In Augustine, however, the problem is human freedom and its capacity to will the good. Grace becomes a power and a force within human existence changing a person's innermost motivation and liberating one's will to delight in God. In Luther the problem is the whole person; grace is the word of God's forgiveness that reckons a person righteous so that he or she is transformed.

35. W. Joest, "Rechtfertigung im ev. Glaubensverstandnis," *Lexikon für Theologie und Kirche* 8 (Freiburg: Herder, 1963): 1047–1049.

36. Luther, *Freedom*, p. 71.

37. Pesch, "Existential and Sapiential Theology," pp. 66–67. Luther writes: "This obedience, however, is not rendered by works, but by faith alone. On the other hand, what greater rebellion against God, what greater wickedness, what greater contempt of God is there than not believing his promise? For what is this but to make God a liar or to doubt that he is truthful?" (*Freedom*, p. 59).

38. Cf. *Summa Theologiae* I–II, 113, 3–5.

39. Cf. *Summa Theologiae* I–II, 114, 3.

40. Gerrish, *Reason and Grace*, pp. 131–133; Pesch, "Existential and Sapiential Theology," p. 67.

41. Gerrish, *Reason and Grace*, p. 133.

42. Pesch, "Existential and Sapiential Theology," p. 67.

43. Cf. Gerrish, *Reason and Grace*, p. 125.

44. Cf. Ibid., pp. 115–118, 126–127, 128, n. 1, 135 and n. 1.

45. Wicks sees some of these tendencies developing in Luther's early theology. Cf. *Yearning*, pp. 273–276.

46. Luther, *Freedom*, p. 61.

47. Søren Kierkegaard, *Concluding Unscientific Postscript*, trans. David Swenson and Walter Lowrie (Princeton: Princeton University Press, 1941), pp. 438–440. Kierkegaard presents the parable here in terms of pagan mythology as a relationship between a god who falls in love with an earthly woman.

48. Cf. Paul Tillich, *Love, Power, and Justice* (New York: A Galaxy Book, Oxford University Press, 1960), pp. 82–86, 121–122.

49. Luther, *Freedom*, p. 63.

50. Paul Tillich, *The Protestant Era* (Chicago: Phoenix Books, The University of Chicago Press, 1957), p. 163.

51. Paul Tillich, *On the Boundary: An Autobiographical Sketch* (New York: Charles Scribner's Sons, 1966), pp. 48, 51.

52. Luther, *Freedom*, p. 73. It may be that this theme became obscured in Luther's later writings and behavior. But this authentic early theme from Luther's writing can be seen as severely modifying any radical split between the "two kingdoms" found in his later thought.

53. Cf. Gerrish, *Grace and Reason*, p. 128, n. 1; p. 135, n. 1.

54. Luther, *Freedom*, pp. 73–74.

55. Dietrich Bonhoeffer, *Letters and Papers from Prison* (New York: The Macmillan Company, Paperbacks Ed., 1962), p. 237.

56. Luther, *The Bondage of the Will*, in Dillenberger, *Martin Luther*, pp. 181, 203.

57. Wicks, "Vision," p. 37.

58. Avery Dulles, *The Survival of Dogma* (Garden City, N.Y.: Doubleday & Co., 1971), p. 24.

59. Luther, *Freedom*, pp. 53–57.

5
Trent: Grace and Justification

Twenty-eight years after the indulgence controversy sparked by Luther, which in turn touched off the Reformation, the Council of Trent convened to formulate the Catholic Church's most considered dogmatic reply to the reformers. In its *Decree on Justification* the council takes up the issues on grace that Luther especially had raised. Because of its comprehensiveness, the *Decree on Justification* is probably the most significant and important of all the Roman Catholic teachings on grace. It contains the definition of basic terms in the officially Roman Catholic language of grace.

History of the Decree

The Council of Trent finally opened on December 13, 1545, with less than thirty bishops in attendance. The number of bishops, who were mostly Italian and Spanish, increased and fluctuated during the first period of the council, which lasted until March 1547.[1] The initial discussions were given over to planning the council's program and its concrete order of procedure. By February 1546 it was decided to treat both doctrinal and practical reform matters simultaneously and to begin with the question of Scriptures. On April 8, during the fourth session, with the number of bishops having almost doubled, the council issued its first major decrees, one *On Sacred Scripture and Tradition*, the other *On the Vulgate Edition of the Bible*. And on June 17, during the fifth session, the council proclaimed its *Decree on Original Sin*. It was ready then to turn to the more difficult question of justification and grace. The task would prove to be arduous; it took seven months of work before *The Decree on Justification* was finally approved.

The problem was manifold. The council was aware that it was defining doctrine anew, and the Fathers realized the significance and importance of this decree. Compared with Scholasticism, the doctrine of grace had been cast in a new light by Luther and the Lutherans with their emphasis on sin and their focus on justification. There were no ready answers in Church tradition and doctrine that could be simply cited in response.[2] "If the Council was to be in a position to issue an authentic, dogmatic statement of the content of the Catholic faith, and to define the boundaries that separate it from the Lutheran theory of salvation, it was bound to undertake intensive preliminary work in the theological sphere."[3] Internally there were the differences among the theological schools to be reckoned with on certain key issues. And externally, political considerations and the outbreak of war proved to be distractions.

The council began its work by submitting to its theologians in June a schema of questions concerning the main issues that Luther had raised: the total gratuity of grace, the internal effects of grace, the meaning of *sola fide* and the nature of faith, human cooperation with the process of justification, certitude concerning grace and salvation, the question of merit.[4] During the course of the early discussions of these questions some basic decisions were made. The council would not excerpt texts from the reformers' writings and condemn them but would try to get to the heart of the matter by treating justification objectively and comprehensively.[5] But at the same time their precise focus would be to delimit Catholic understanding over against that of the reformers. Thus when different understandings of the matter stemming from the schools appeared, especially differences between the Scotists and the Thomists, the council would not attempt to solve these problems. They limited themselves to defining and condemning non-Catholic positions.

A first draft of a decree was submitted to the Council on July 23–24. But the council fathers were distracted at this time because of the proximity of the war against the Protestant princes. Moreover the issue of transferring the council to a new site also became more urgent. And when debate on the draft was begun in August it was found unacceptable, especially because of its excessive length and unclear style. It was judged that an entirely new draft should be submitted, in fact, one was already prepared.[6]

On September 23, the council was presented with a new draft of the decree on justification whose anonymous author was Seripando, the superior general of the Augustinians. This draft, however, had itself gone through some preliminary stages in which modifications had been made. Originally, Seripando's draft contained the doctrine of a twofold or double justification, provisional in this life and definitive at the moment of final judgment. This was removed and expressly rejected in the "September draft" presented to the council fathers. But Seripando reintroduced the idea of the twofold justice in the debate on the draft and it was treated at length by the theologians during October. The results of these discussions were most important and they will deserve special attention further on.

As a result of the work of the conciliar theologians and of the debate on general congregations during October, the September draft was modified into the November draft, which in turn was revised still more. It

> was subjected to a fresh scrutiny, chapter by chapter, canon by canon, in eight general congregations held between 7 and 17 December. Not content with this, the legates convened those of the bishops who were also trained theologians for the purpose of once more examining with them every important aspect of the problem, so as to make sure of the assent of the plenary assembly. This small, expert circle of episcopal theologians held no less than eighteen conferences.[7]

This work was finished in early January, just in time for the scheduled sixth session on January 13, 1547, when the *Decree on Justification* was approved unanimously by the council fathers.

Situating the Decree

Because Trent's *Decree on Justification* is the most comprehensive of the Roman Catholic church's teachings on grace, it becomes especially important to situate it historically and to recognize its limitations. These can be seen from several points of view.

Jedin writes: "The Tridentine decree on justification is the Church's authoritative answer to the teaching of Luther and the *Confessio Augustana* on grace and justification."[8] And in Luther, the question of justification assumed an enormous importance; it is close to the center of his language of grace. The council, then, adapted itself to Luther, and set its teaching in the context of sin (chap. 1), and this marks the first limiting factor of its teaching on grace. To make justification central in one's teaching on grace is to make sin central. The teaching of Trent, then, must be set against the background of Scripture and a whole tradition of the understanding of grace. The grace of Christ must be situated in the whole mystery and economy of creation and redemption. The effects of grace must be seen to be as complex and polyvalent as the role of Christ himself and as rich and manifold as Christian life. Any attempt to express the mystery of grace must be situated in a context of a historical tradition that far exceeds the question of justification.[9]

It follows that the whole of Catholic teaching cannot be found in any one place. And for this reason, the teaching of Trent on the question of justification itself is also limited. These limitations are not difficult to pinpoint. The primary intention of the council fathers was to define *over against* what they took to be Lutheran positions. This cannot be insisted upon too much: The underlying purpose of the decree is to define boundaries, to accentuate that which is different in the two understandings of justification. "The Council's aim was to draw a line of demarcation between Catholic dogma and belief and Protestant teaching."[10] So strong was this concern that even words and phrases that sounded Lutheran were often avoided simply on that account.[11] What was important at this time was to accent differences; "a later epoch might then look once more for connecting lines."[12] Differences between the Catholic schools were accommodated as long as a formula that condemned a Protestant position could be agreed upon. Thus Jedin says: "It is therefore a safe rule for an interpretation of the decree that it must always start from this delimiting function, that is, from the canons."[13] This delimiting function thus becomes a limitation of the decree itself; in spite of its attempt at comprehensiveness, there is a one-sidedness of concern, approach and statement. "The exclusively anti-Gnostic, anti-Arian, anti-Lutheran, anti-Modernist position is not the representative Catholic position."[14]

This one-sidedness is manifest particularly in two areas, both of which are important for an understanding of the decree. The first is a stress on the human person and what happens to the person in the process of justification. Theocentrism and a heightened emphasis on God's transcendence and sovereignty are basic to Luther's theology. This presents at least the danger of extrinsicism. Over against this, on one point after another, the counter themes of what God does for the person and what human existence can do under God's grace are accented in the decree. In a sense this is to be expected, therefore, and it might be said that from a higher point of view Trent supplements or complements the Lutheran weight on "God alone."[15]

Second, to a certain extent Scholastic terminology was dropped in the decree and scriptural texts are cited in abundance. But at the same time, the framers of the decree, both bishops and theologians, were trained in Scholasticism. The Augustinians present did not get their way too often. In fact, then, many Scholastic suppositions are present in the decree and help to explain the positions taken. In *this* sense, namely, "that the decree rests on the results of scholastic theology,"[16] its language is Scholastic and embodies many of its limitations. And for this reason, also, many of the broad differences between the Lutheran and Scholastic languages of grace, their different stress and methods and points of view, are embodied in the decree.

In spite of its limitations, however, the *Decree on Justification* is a remarkable document both for its clarity and tempered nuance. This is so much the case that Harnack could not resist the following speculation:

> The decree on justification, though an artificial product, is in many respects an excellent piece of work; in fact one may doubt whether the Reformation would have developed if this decree had been issued by the Lateran Council, at the opening of the century, and had really passed into the Church's flesh and blood.[17]

The Teaching of Trent

The following summary of the basic teachings of Trent on justification and grace touches only on central affirmations, and some of these are more central than others. It is merely a summary, following in general the order of the decree itself.

Human beings cannot be justified by the power of nature. In the first chapter and the first three canons, the council reaffirms the doctrine of Carthage and Second Orange: There is an absolute need of grace for justification. Negatively, human existence cannot be justified by the power of its nature, by its works, by the Law of Moses, without grace. Nor can we turn toward God without grace. These positions are shared with the reformers, so that like them the council begins with the helplessness of humanity in sin.

Justification is a real remission of sins. Trent defines justification as a passing from one state of being to another, from the state into which one is born, into the state of grace and adoption as children of God (chap. 4). Christ's death is an objective redemption or justification for the sins of all people (chap. 2). This is received subjectively by particular persons through grace. In baptism, Original Sin is really remitted. This does not mean that concupiscence does not remain; it does, but it is not properly called sin and does not harm one who resists it.[18]

Justification is also a sanctification and interior renovation of the person. This is the core of Trent's doctrine of justification and it is found in chapter 7. "Justification is not only the remission of sins." It is also "sanctification and renovation of the interior man . . . whereby a man becomes just instead of unjust" (chap. 7 and c. 11). This justification is called a rebirth, which is effected by grace (chap. 3), by an infusion of grace and charity that is poured forth into a person's heart by the Holy Spirit (c. 11). It should be noted that this is meant to exclude not the idea of imputation, but of "mere" imputation or "remission of sin alone," that is, the idea that there is no inner change in a person (cf. c. 11). The point, then, is that with this interior renovation we *are made* just, and *become* just or righteous before God; we *are* justified (chaps. 3 and 7). This realism of the effect of grace and the process of justification has the strong accent it does because of the Scholastic supposition of created grace, which, however, is never mentioned. In common terms the justified person becomes a new being living a new life.

This process of justification involves a free acceptance on the part of a person. Human beings are active and cooperate with grace through stages of preparation for justification. This accent on the free will and cooperation of human beings with grace is announced very early in the decree, in chapter 1; in spite of sin, the free will of a person is not destroyed. In the adult, the process of justification is a conscious and voluntary reception of grace (chap. 7). Thus when grace moves a person, he or she cooperates by a free assent. In chapter 5, the necessity of this cooperation is noted. All begins with God's prevenient grace, a call. With this unmerited call, human existence is awakened and assisted and is thus made ready for justification. In this process, one is active under the influence of grace. After all, the council says, "he certainly does something, since he could reject it" (chap. 5).

In chapter 6, the decree goes on to give a concrete psychological description of this preparation-cooperation, of the many-faceted way in which a person becomes active under grace in becoming ready to receive justifying grace. One hears and believes; accepts revelation as true; fears God's justice; hopes and is confident in God's promise; begins to love God; begins to hate sin; determines to receive baptism, to lead a new life, to keep the commandments. These dispositions on the part of a person mark an active cooperation with grace.

These assertions are meant to counter two points in Luther's theology. The first is the idea that faith is purely passive or that human existence remains purely passive under the influence of grace. The second point is one aspect of the *sola fide* doctrine. The council says that other dispositions are also necessary (c. 9). In chapter 7 it is stated that faith without hope or without charity does not unite a person to God. Thus it sometimes appears in the decree as if faith were only one of the preparatory acts or dispositions leading to salvation.[19]

It might be well to point out here that the rejection of the formula *sola fide* in the decree is not an out-and-out rejection of the doctrine. It is rather, as Küng tells us, a rejection of a very particular understanding of it (c. 9). In fact, Küng points out that Aquinas too used the formula.[20] It should be recalled that in Luther the phrase *sola fide* tends to mean the same as *sola gratia*; one receives all from God's grace because human existence is totally incapable of self-justification. On the other side, however, Catholic theology has tended to give much more emphasis to charity than the reformers, especially after Augustine and Aquinas made the distinction between dead faith (or belief) and faith informed with love.

The justice of justified persons is their own. This affirmation appears in chapter 7. It is central to Catholic understanding and appears as a mere corollary of the realism of the effect of justification, that is, that a person is made really just. Although the Scholastic terms such as "habit" or "created grace" are not used in the decree, they can be seen supporting the notions of "infusion" and "inherent," which are used. There is a great difference here between the decree and the language of Luther. For him a person is just by a *justitia aliena*, by the justice of another, Christ's, and not one's own. The total gratuity of grace means for Luther that human beings of themselves have precisely nothing of their own.

There is not nor can there be absolute certitude concerning the state of grace, perseverance or salvation. No other issue caused more debate, discussion and controversy than this one. At the bottom of the discussions were different notions of the meaning of faith, especially between the Thomists and Scotists. Twice the council decided not to solve the issue between the different Scholastic opinions, and to address themselves exclusively to condemning the proposition of the Lutherans that a certitude of grace, forgiveness and salvation is essentially part of the faith that saves. Finally, as late as January 9, 1547, four days before the final approval of the decree, an acceptable formula was found and it was approved on January 11. "No one can know with the certitude of faith, which cannot admit of any error, that he has obtained God's grace" (chap. 9). In all, it is not the objective certitude of God's promise or of the efficacy of the sacraments that is in question here, but rather the religious fear that stems from recognizing personal human weakness and our defective dispositions (chap. 9). Moreover, certitude about one's own salvation is considered presumption (chap. 12). It should be noted that in all of this the notion or meaning of faith, how it is understood, is the issue on which everything hangs.

It is possible and necessary to obey the law. In asserting this, the council attacks the idea of *faith alone* again, this time in the context of faith and works. In chapter 10, it affirms that human beings, through acts of virtue, advance in justification: Justice in a person increases through a faith that plays itself out in good works. In chapter 11, then, the council affirms that the Christian is *bound* to observe the law, both of God and of the Church (c. 20). With God's grace the justified person *can* obey the law and it is necessary for him or her to do so.

Two comments are apropos here. The first regards the increase of justification. Luther tended to think of justification as *all at once*, something that occurs now in the existential contact with God through faith in Christ; we are justified and saved now. The reasons for this emphasis are clear enough, but the result is that he did not clearly distinguish between *justification* and *sanctification*. Neither did the council take account of this distinction. The confusion that arises from the lack of distinction and the intermingling of these two concepts, that is, being made just and increasing in sanctification, leads to oppositions that are not really necessary. Later on, Calvin was to make a clear distinction between justification and sanctification in his *Institutes*.[21]

Second, regarding the possibility of observing the law, the council admits that no matter how holy a person is, he or she will still commit slight daily sins (chaps. 11 and c. 23). Along with the Sixteenth Council of Carthage (418, against Pelagius) and other considerations, Küng makes this a basis for a Catholic doctrine of *simul justus et peccator*.[22]

Justification is lost by any mortal sin. Once received, the grace of justification can be driven out of life by any mortal sin and not just by loss of faith. On the other hand, people can sin mortally, lose their justice, while their faith can remain. This is the teaching of chapter 15 and can be seen as yet another attack on the idea of *faith alone*. The Scholastic notion of faith underlies this conception as well as grace as an inherent state of being that is infused.

In chapter 14, the council teaches that if justification is lost by mortal sin, it may be regained again through repentance and through sacramental confession, or the desire for it. It should be noticed that both one's initial justification and one's regaining of the grace of justice after personal sin are in the Catholic understanding very closely connected with the sacraments. Initial justification is received through baptism, the sacrament of faith (chap. 7). After personal sin, justification cannot be regained by faith alone without reference to the sacrament of reconciliation, at least in desire (c. 29).

One truly merits salvation through good works in grace. This is asserted in chapter 16, which deals with the nature of merit and how it works in the economy of the Christian life. Once again the council rejects the idea of faith alone. Good works in the Christian life carry the idea of cooperating with grace in such a way that salvation can be considered a "reward," and one that is "truly merited." The strong affirmations of merit in this chapter mark a significant difference between the Protestant and the Catholic languages of grace. But they are counterbalanced by other considerations in the same chapter that will be seen in what immediately follows.

Problems in Trent's Language of Grace

As can be seen, the Tridentine language of grace shares many of the insights and the limitations of Scholasticism. But two problems in particular stand out, especially when the position of Trent is contrasted with that of the reformers, and something should be said about them.

If the justified person has a justice that becomes his or her *own* and that is not identical with the justice of Christ, is not the total gratuity of salvation compromised (cf. c. 10)? In other words, in this case is a person's justification and salvation really had through Christ *alone*? The problem appears when the Catholic position is contrasted with that of the typically Protestant position. The Protestant will tend to say that when we sinners appear before God we will not have a justice that is *our own*. It will be the justice of Christ. Only in this way, he will say, is the *total* gratuity of justification guaranteed.

A response to this problem will help in the understanding of the Tridentine language of grace. It can be approached in two ways, first, theologically, and, second, historically.

Theologically, the notion of inherent justice is clearly related to the notion of habitual grace, an inherent form in the person giving one a new mode of spiritual being and a disposition for supernatural acts. This habitual grace is often conceived of by Protestant theologians as giving human existence some power or autonomy before God. This is a misconception. The study of the evolution of the concept and its use in Aquinas shows that the notion of habit emerged precisely to affirm and to ensure that it is not a human being's natural power that is eliciting a salvific act, but a supernatural power from God's grace.[23] This justice inhering in the person, therefore, means that God has a hold on our being and that we are supernaturally dependent on him. It signifies not autonomy before God but dependence on his grace.[24].

Second, historically and doctrinally two points can be made from the decree itself. The first is the fact that the decree affirms that God alone is the efficient cause of justification. God alone and not human beings effects human justification and salvation (chap. 7).

But second and more important is the conception that appears in chapter 16 and that was decided during the October discussions concerning Seripando's notion of double or twofold justice. Seripando suggested, as some theologians had before him, that although a person was really justified in this world, in the moment of death that person must yet make a final appeal to the justice of Christ, for only the imputation of this perfect justice could make one worthy of salvation. This idea was rejected because logically it undermined the whole concept of a person's being really made just at all in the process of justification. But at the same time, it was insisted that although one's justice becomes one's own, as the Scholastics' language demanded, this justice could not be separated from the justice of Christ. The inherent justice that sanctifying grace effects is precisely an ontological union with Christ, a communion between head and members. The possession of sanctifying grace is a participation in Christ's justice.[25] This notion, Jedin says, is the most important positive understanding hammered out in the discussions after Seripando's draft was submitted in September of 1546.[26] The concept appears in chapter 16 where the justified person is presented as united with Christ in the mystical language of John and Paul. There the decree explicitly states that in saying justice becomes one's own, God's justice is not to be neglected or disregarded; rather, the justice that inheres in a person is also God's justice. The just person is a living member of Christ (c. 32). This idea of participation, then, is not unlike Luther's own conception of the union of the sinner with the bridegroom Christ, even though it is expressed in very different terms.

The second problem concerns merit. If a person must cooperate with grace in order to be justified (chap. 5, c. 4), and in such a way that salvation can be said to be "truly merited" and called a reward (chap. 16), is not salvation "conditioned" by human response? Is it not therefore dependent also on human beings? And consequently are not the total transcendence and sovereignty of God and our total dependence on him for salvation undermined?

In response it must be said that human cooperation with grace cannot be conceived synergistically. It is not to be imagined as two forces working together on the same level, like two people pulling on the same rope. Nor can this cooperation be conceived of in such a way that God is pictured as waiting on human response; our active response to grace cannot be said to condition God's initiative, efficacy or judgment. These are the anthropomorphisms to which the language of cooperation and merit is certainly open.

And yet the freedom of human existence must be preserved and affirmed. As Aquinas said, God deals with human beings according to their free and conscious nature. But in affirming this in rather strong language, the decree is equally strong in introducing the dialectical element of dependence. In chapter 16 it says that God's grace always precedes, accompanies and follows. His gifts are our merits. And psychologically, no one should have confidence in oneself but should rely totally on God. These are the very religious concerns of Luther that have found their way into the decree.

Ultimately, one has here the elements of the mystery involved in the relation between God and human existence. In the end, this dialogue between God's sovereign power and human freedom in connection with salvation collapses into mystery before all analysis. At least the *de auxiliis* controversies at the end of the century tend to show that this cannot be fully worked out in terms of the mechanisms of ontological systems.

Conclusion

In conslusion it might be asked whether there is a possibility of a rapprochement between the Roman Catholic and Protestant languages of grace. In this regard, Hans Küng's *Justification* is certainly a brilliant milestone. Karl Barth, a "neo-Calvinist" and probably the most influential Protestant theologian of the twentieth century, has recognized Küng's presentation of his own position as completely accurate, and has accepted Küng's presentation of the Catholic position as compatible with his own thought and as acceptable to himself. And most Catholic interpreters have recognized Küng's presentation of Catholic doctrine as truly Catholic and orthodox.[27] The work thus represents in fact a rapprochement in which, as Küng says, the differences are no more than those that existed among the schools.[28]

But from a different point of view, it might be asked whether a common language of grace is really something to be desired. Each different language of grace has its own ability to highlight certain aspects of the mystery of grace and thus helps to uncover its richness in a way that others cannot. Would it not be better to have a plurality of languages of grace? Of course this would mean a pluralism in doctrine because of the fact that different languages have their own internal logic and, as has been seen, arrive at different conclusions. Thus one would have to recognize a pluralism of doctrine in which different doctrines would be considered equally valid.

Ultimately it would seem that these two approaches do not have to be exclusive. From a "higher point of view" one can often see agreements and construct expressions of them that show forth and articulate a unity of faith. This is the point of ecumenical discussion among Christians. At the same time, however, one can admit the integrity of different doctrinal positions in their limited perspectives. Such a doctrinal pluralism would recognize that there are different valid experiences of Christ's grace and so there must be different doctrines and spiritualities typical of different Christian groups or churches.

Notes

1. The council continued intermittently over 18 years up to December 1563 in Bologna (1547–1549) and Trent (1551–1552 and 1562–1563).
2. Hubert Jedin, *A History of the Council of Trent*, vol. II, trans. Ernest Graf (St. Louis: B. Herder Book Co., 1961), pp. 167, 309.
3. Ibid., pp. 169–170.
4. Ibid., pp. 170–171. Luther of course did not question the total gratuity of grace but insisted on it with great emphasis.
5. Ibid., p. 174.
6. Ibid., pp. 195–196.
7. Ibid., p. 293.
8. Ibid., p. 307.
9. Hans Küng, *Justification: The Doctrine of Karl Barth and a Catho-*

lic Reflection (New York: Thomas Nelson & Sons, 1964), p. 214. Cf. also pp. 99–122.

10. Jedin, *Trent*, p. 309.

11. Cf. ibid., p. 295.

12. Ibid., p. 260.

13. Ibid., p. 309.

14. Karl Adam, cited by Küng, *Justification*, p. 104.

15. Ibid., p. 106.

16. Jedin, *Trent*, p. 309.

17. Cited by Jedin, *Trent*, p. 310.

18. Cf. Trent's "Decree on Original Sin," *The Church Teaches*, ed. and trans. by John Clarkson et al. (St. Louis: B. Herder Book Co., 1955), pp. 158–161.

19. Seripando reacted strongly against this tendency. Cf. Jedin, *Trent*, p. 285. In all of this it should not be assumed that Trent interpreted Luther correctly or adequately.

20. Küng, *Justification*, p. 250.

21. "Of central importance is the distinction introduced by Calvin between justification and sanctification. This distinction was not taken into consideration in the definitions of Trent. The council was satisfied to affirm in regard to *justification* a series of things which the Reformation refused to admit, preferring to attribute them instead to *sanctification*" (Charles Moeller, cited by Küng, *Justification*, p. 270). Cf. also Brian Gerrish, *Grace and Reason* (Oxford: Clarendon Press, 1962), p. 135, n. 1.

Calvin deals with sanctification, that is, repentance, new life in the Spirit, and the Christian life in Book III, chapters 3–10 of the *Institutes of the Christian Religion*, ed. John T. McNeil (Philadelphia: Westminster Press, 1960). Here one sees a language of grace and spirituality that is much closer to that of Roman Catholicism than that of Luther. At the same time, however, the basic structure of Luther's doctrine of justification by faith is preserved intact by Calvin.

22. Cf. Küng, pp. 236–248.

23. Cf. *supra*, pp. 59–60, 66–67. The point is that if there were no supernatural habit as the principle of an act of love, it would be an act of human nature, thus giving persons a power for their own salvation. The same is true of the other virtues that are rooted in habitual grace.

24. Cf. J.P. Kenny, *The Supernatural* (New York: Alba House, 1972), p. 48; Küng, *Justification*, p. 206; Henri Bouillard, *Conversion et grâce chez St. Thomas d'Aquin* (Paris: Aubier, 1944), pp. 160–161, 219.

25. Jedin, *Trent*, pp. 255–256.

26. Ibid., p. 308.

27. Cf. Karl Rahner, "Questions of Controversial Theology on Justification," *Theological Investigations* IV (Baltimore: Helicon Press, 1966), pp. 189–218, where he discusses Küng's work.

28. Küng, *Justification*, p. xiii.

6
Rahner: Grace and History

Born in 1904 in Freiburg, Germany, Karl Rahner entered the Jesuit order at the age of 18. During his early study of philosophy, besides his regular courses, Rahner read carefully both Kant and the works of Joseph Marechal, a Belgian Jesuit philosopher. Upon finishing his Jesuit course of training in 1934, Rahner began doctoral studies in philosopy at the University of Freiburg. There he participated in the seminar of Martin Heidegger and at the same time wrote an interpretative thesis on the metaphysics of knowledge in Aquinas. The thesis, however, was not accepted, apparently because it was not a strictly historical work. Thus after two years at Freiburg Rahner went to Innsbruck, rapidly prepared a historical study on the Fathers, and became a Doctor of Theology in December, 1936.

Rahner began his teaching career with the course on grace and continued to develop that course in the years that followed. In the summer of 1937, he was invited to give lectures at the Salzburg summer school on the "Foundations of a Philosophy of Religion." In 1939, he published his original thesis on Aquinas as *Geist in Welt, Spirit in the World*.[1] And then, in 1941, the lectures he had given on the philosophy of religion were put together as the book *Hörer des Wortes, Hearers of the Word*.[2] These two works form the philosophical and anthropological foundations for Rahner's work in theology.

The interpretation of Rahner's theology of grace that follows is a particularly limited one. First of all it will treat Rahner's main ideas historically, that is, how they unfolded in only a few of his major articles.[3] Then, too, it will focus on the question of grace and history, especially as that problem is dealt with in Rahner's three articles on salvation history found in *Theological Investigations*, volume 5. Before this, however, we venture to present three basic ideas of Rahner's thought that continually recur and give his theology something of a systematic character.

Some Basic Notions

The first fundamental notion in Rahner's highly technical language is his idea of the transcendence of the human spirit and *how*, even though it is bound to sensible data and to this world, it can come in contact with "absolute being." In his analysis of human knowing in *Spirit in the World*, Rahner shows that the human mind can grasp the whole realm of being as finite, and that in so doing it comes in contact with infinity. One can only grasp that the totality of beings is finite against a "horizon," or "background," or "field" of infinity. Limitedness stands out only against an implicit grasp of the unlimited. In *Hearers of the Word* Rahner expands his analysis of human existence and sees it as fundamentally oriented toward God, but in such a way that God can really be "known" only by being encountered in the world and through history. Human being is transcendence and at the same time an "awaiter" of God's word addressed to it in this world and in history.

What is perhaps more important here is the way Rahner goes about establishing these things. He begins with human acts themselves and examines their inherent suppositions. By this "transcendental" analysis he tries to uncover the necessary underlying structure of overt behavior; he attempts to establish the necessary conditions (of the possibility) that must be present for any act to take place at all, and therefore that are present in every similar act. This necessary structure of human spiritual operations is thus called a priori, that is, something necessarily implied in every spiritual act. In his analyses, then, Rahner establishes the implicit transcendence in every spiritual act of a human being. Such an act is a tendency toward and a contact with absolute being, that can be uncovered by analysis, and that also appears in consciousness as an a priori horizon or background, but that is never grasped as an object. Human transcendence is simply an "openness," an outward reach, an *excessus*, whose object can be experienced only in an "implicit," "preconceptual" (not objective) and "unthematic" way.

A second fundamental notion in Rahner's theology is his conception of grace. By grace God offers himself personally to human beings, he gives himself to human existence. In ontological terms, God communicates himself by way of quasi-formal causality. Many of Rahner's most important contributions to theology stem from developments of this conception of grace. But this will be dealt with below.

And third, perhaps the most important principle of all in Rahner's theology comes ultimately from Aristotle's and Aquinas's hylomorphism: the theory of matter and form, or more generally of act and potency. Rahner has adapted this into a formal principle to show how things can be radically distinct and at the same time intimately united and one. This is best illustrated in the human person where the human soul is taken as the substantial "form" giving shape and substance to human "matter." The unity of matter and spirit in the human person, as well as their radical distinction, can be seen in the dialectical and paradoxical statements that can be made about the human person. Spirit is not matter; by definition matter is non-spirit. And a person's spirit is *not* his or her body. Yet a person's body *is* the presence of the spirit, and one *is* one's body. Spirit and matter are radically different and yet they are one in being because they cause each other to be. Matter determines spirit by being that which spirit informs; spirit informs this matter making it to be what it is. They are one because they are mutually or reciprocally causative of each other.[4]

This ontologically grounded principle of simultaneous identity or unity and distinction and diversity (plurality) runs all through Rahner's theology and is particularly operative in his theology of grace. For the human spirit in its transcendence is a "potency" for receiving the supernatural, grace, God's self-gift. And grace is related as form or act to a person's transcendence, which is "matter" or an active potency to receive it. Thus, once given, supernatural grace becomes an intimate part of human reality, even while remaining radically distinct from it. With this understanding of the identity of grace with the operation of the transcendence of the human spirit, Rahner can explain the operation of grace in terms of an analysis of human self-transcendence in consciousness, freedom and moral behavior.

Redefining the Notion of Grace

In 1939 Rahner wrote his ground-breaking article "Some Implications of the Scholastic Concept of Uncreated Grace."[5] The background of the article is clearly stated by Fransen. During the centur-
ies that followed Trent, "theologians satisfied themselves mainly
with substantiating the existence of created grace. By and large, they
failed to give serious thought to what is in fact the ultimate root of
man's interior sanctification: the living indwelling of the Blessed Trin-
ity. And so created grace was understood by the ordinary faithful to
be the thing in itself."[6] Scholastic theologians agreed that through
grace one entered into a new relationship with God, but they taught
that this relationship was based on an entative or ontological change
in the human person. In so doing they seemed to subordinate God's
presence to existence; his indwelling, to this created change in a
person's being. The problem, however, is that Scripture (especially
Paul and John) seems to contradict this. There grace appears as first
and foremost a communication of the personal Spirit of God who
thus becomes present to human being personally. The created effect
within a person is precisely an effect or consequence of this indwelling and not the other way around.[7]

Rahner redefines the primacy of uncreated grace by arguing
from a conception of the beatific vision. Lest it seem strange that a
theologian try to show the way things are on earth from the way they
are in heaven, two things should be noted. First, Scholastic tradition
itself had taught that being-in-grace and the *visio* of God are continuous; ontologically, the same union with God in glory is shared in a
hidden and rudimentary way through grace.[8] And second, theology
is an attempt to understand. Thus it is not altogether absurd to cast
one's understanding of a union with God through grace against the
background of the closest possible union with him imaginable, that
is, a theology of the *visio*.

In Rahner's conception, knowledge is characterized as being-
present-to-itself. A human being as conscious knower is a being-
reflected-upon-itself. A person knows reality outside the self through
the means of a *species impressa*, that is, "an ontological determination of the knower as an entity in his own reality."[9] The person,
reflecting on the self under the influence of reality outside the self but
determining the self interiorly, is aware of him or her self and knows

the outside world precisely as other than the self. In the *visio*, however, God's own being and reality take the place of this *species*. The *visio* is a direct vision, a union without created intermediary, a spiritual union in which God gives himself to the knower. Ontologically, God presents himself to the blessed through quasi-formal causality.[10] The created effect of this in human existence is a being flooded with the "light of glory." This effect is related to God's being-present-to-man as matter is to form. This means that this *lumen gloriae* is only there as an added ultimate disposition (or "material cause") through God's being present by "informing."

This structure of God's being present to human existence in the *visio* is made the model for Rahner's understanding of grace. In ontological terms, grace is primarily God communicating himself to human beings in the mode of formal causality. Created grace is secondary; it can exist only to the extent that God's formal causality is actually being exercised, and as an ultimate disposition for that exercise.[11]

The highly technical and ontological language of Rahner should not be allowed to obscure the significance of his position. In this theoretical understanding, Rahner has first of all reestablished, in terms acceptable to Scholasticism, that the primary meaning of grace is God's presence to and indwelling within the human person. Second, this ontological account really transcends itself. That is to say, it explains why one can, should and must use personalist language in describing grace and its effects.[12] Rahner himself consistently describes grace as God's gift of himself to human beings, his personal self-donation to the person in love. And, third, in this ontology of God's efficient creative causality and his "supernatural" quasi-formal causality, one has a framework for understanding the world and history in terms of a dialogue with God. The world and finite spirits are created by God as distinct and radically other than himself. And God enters into interpersonal dialogue with human beings precisely as other, by freely offering them his love and asking for a free response of love. In fact, this communication in grace is the very reason for creation.[13]

Nature and Grace

In 1950 Rahner addressed the extrinsicist view of the relation between nature and grace that had long plagued Catholic theology and the seeds of which can be seen in Scholasticism itself.[14] The context of this article, "Concerning the Relationship between Nature and Grace,"[15] is the conflicting views of the so-called *nouvelle théologie* of de Lubac and Bouillard and others, who had just been embarrassed by the encyclical "Humani Generis" (1950), and Scholastic extrinsicism. Rahner accepts the concerns of the *nouvelle théologie*, but proposes his own highly original and very significant solution to the problem with his doctrine of the "supernatural existential."

The problem to which Rahner is responding should be clearly drawn. In stressing the clear and radical distinction between the natural and supernatural orders, Scholastic language opened the way to a view in which these two orders appeared as separate and self-enclosed spheres of reality. The extrinsicist conception of nature is that of an autonomous and closed system, in which human nature was effectively reduced to a "pure nature," devoid of anything supernatural and of any experience of it. In this view the supernatural order of revelation and grace is conceived of as being imposed on human existence by an external decree of God, completely from outside nature, outside history, outside human experience. The connection of this religious sphere to a person's life is essentially one of authority and obedience. The apologetic and religious consequences of this view are most significant. If the human person is completely at home in the self-enclosed natural world, there is no reason or need why one should look for or be interested in a revelation. And should such a religious revelation be accepted, it will appear as a disturbance of our natural life and external force binding our freedom. Such a supernatural revelation will be completely unintelligible, but blindly obeyed, because it will respond to no need or desire grounded in natural experience and life in this world.[16]

To overcome extrinsicism, the New Theology exploited the Augustinian idea of the natural ordination of human existence toward and desire for God, which appears in Aquinas as a natural desire to see God. In doing so, however, it seemed to the critics of this movement that the gratuity of grace and the supernatural order was undermined. For in Scholastic language, and on the supposition of the immutability of God, if there is an inner ordination to grace and the supernatural order that is part of human nature as such, since natures are ordained to their goal by teleological necessity, God could not refuse a human being grace without contradicting his creative intention. The total gratuity of grace and salvation would be undermined then becaue it would seem that grace was owed to this natural desire and ordination.[17]

Rahner poses his solution to the problem not by analyzing human existence but by arguing theologically from the universal salvific will of God. God in his redemptive will has called all human beings to salvation, and this binding ordination of all people to a supernatural end cannot remain simply a decree external to human existence. An ontology that grasps that concrete quiddity of human existence depends utterly on God will realize as well that God's binding disposition for people constitutes what humanity *is*.

> If God gives creation and man above all a supernatural end and this end is first "in intentione," then man (and the world) *is* by that very fact always and everywhere inwardly other in structure than he would be if he did not have this end, and hence other as well before he has reached this end partially (the grace which justifies) or wholly (the beatific vision).[18]

The supernatural existential, then, refers to the actual concrete situation of the human world and history. It is the fact that this has been raised up to a supernatural level, from the beginning, by the gracious, gratuitous and supernatural call of God of created reality back to himself.[19]

But the supernatural existential can also be approached descriptively. After establishing the fact of this concrete situation, Rahner describes more concretely the consequences and the working out of this existential situation. In *Spirit in the World* and *Hearers of the Word*, Rahner had thoroughly analyzed the transcendence of the human spirit. Spirit opens up toward absolute being and this is a real potency or capacity to receive God's personal self-communication in love. Moreover, this is no mere passive ability to receive grace; it is an active seeking and desiring. But in the light of the supernatural existential, this dynamism appears to be much more than a dynamism of nature; this desire and need is itself a gift, and although not of itself "saving grace," still a supernatural grace.[20] In fact, Rahner says, because of the universal call to salvation (the supernatural existential), in the concrete there is no pure nature. Theologically, one must say that "nature" is simply that which remains when one mentally subtracts the movement, orientation and dynamism that is supernatural.[21] Thus, concretely, the supernatural existential means that all people, quite apart from "verbal" revelation and explicit Christianity, are drawn and driven by a desire for the supernatural and for the immediate vision of God. This active teleological ordination toward grace and salvation, however, is itself a grace.

The brilliance of Rahner's construction here is that it allows one to overcome extrinsicism and to view concrete nature as having an inner desire and need for the supernatural. All he adds is that this inner exigency is itself a gift of grace. It may appear at first sight that this is merely theological sleight of hand, a Rahnerian twist to render the New Theology acceptable to Scholastics. But it is not merely that. Behind Rahner's conception is a whole theology of creation and the Logos that will be touched on below in connection with grace and history.[22] The significance of the doctrine of the supernatural existential is that it opens the way to many other important theological insights for Christian self-understanding.

Conscious Experience of Grace

In the same article of 1950, Rahner took up the question of the consciousness of grace, once again over against Scholastic extrinsicism.[23] Scholasticism assumed that what human beings experience in this world is simply nature.[24] In the Scholastic view, grace and the operation of grace do not enter into consciousness. "Nature alone and its acts are the components of the life which we experience as our own." Grace and all that belongs to the supernatural realm are purely "ontic" structures, components of being, and do not enter into natural human or psychological experience. The result is that nature and grace (the supernatural) are seen as two layers of reality that scarcely penetrate each other. Grace thus has no part in a person's everyday experience of concrete living.[25]

Rahner's view of the experience of grace is a corollary of the theory of the supernatural existential. In brief, he says, first, that grace is experienced, but not as grace; it is indistinguishable from the stirrings of the transcendence of the human spirit. And, second, a person's experience of the supernatural call and address of God is never a perception or grasp of an object; grace appears rather as an unthematic horizon of transcendence.

First, because of the actual elevation of the created order of nature, and the actual call of every person to salvation, all people live in an a priori state of supernaturally elevated spiritual existence; everyone always lives "consciously" in the presence of the triune God. There is always and in every person the possibility of supernatural and salutary acts effected through grace. Actual grace need not be considered as intermittent impulses from God, but may be thought of as a constant offer and possibility arising out of the situation of the supernatural existential itself. In his concrete situation, actual human nature "is continually being determined (which does not mean justified) by the supernatural grace of salvation offered it."[26] Nature and the supernatural are distinct, but they interpenetrate each other, so that pure nature simply does not exist and what is experienced in consciousness is also grace. Self-transcending and religious experience is the experience of grace, but not *as* grace, simply because the movement and dynamism of nature and of the supernatural orientation of this nature by God to himself are indistinguishable. Although distinct, they are one.

Second, the how and where of the experience of grace is described by Rahner concretely in terms of a person's experience of his or her own spiritual transcendence. Human spirit *is* transcendence; it is a capacity for an active openness to the infinite and absolute. And the term or "whither" of this openness can be located. This is not to be taken in the sense that an infinite and absolute object can be experienced, but by analysis it can be shown that contact with absolute being is a condition for or a priori basis for ordinary human spiritual activities. In certain situations, this self-transcending ground of our being and activity becomes especially conscious, but not through a sensible perception or an objective and conceptual knowledge. Awareness of one's own transcendence appears in the "corner of the eye" as a horizon or a field in which the spirit operates. One has an unthematic or preconceptual awareness that the orientation beyond oneself reaches even to infinity. This transcendence of the spirit, then, can be seen as the vehicle of the operation of grace; in the concrete order this transcendence is a supernatural dynamism that reaches to a supernatural horizon, and implicit awareness of it is a consciousness of grace. And such traditional concepts as "illumination" and "inspiration" have their ontological ground in this grace working in and through natural human transcendence.[27]

This consciousness and experience of grace can be localized and described still more concretely in numerous "boundary" or "limit" experiences where the supernatural call or impulse of grace is especially manifested. Grace is operative in the experience of infinite longings, of radical optimism, of unquenchable discontent, of the torment of the insufficiency of everything attainable, of the radical protest against death, the experience of being confronted with an absolute love precisely where it is lethally incomprehensible and seems to be silent and aloof, the experience of a radical guilt and of a still-abiding hope, and so on. These elements are in fact tributary to that divine force which impels the created spirit—by grace—to an absolute fulfillment. Hence in them grace is experienced as well as the natural being of human life.[28]

The Universal Possibility of Salvation

Drawing out the implications of the unity of the natural and supernatural orders still further, Rahner indicates *how* the universal salvific will of God becomes concretized in all people. Because the salvific will of God cannot remain an abstraction, one must say that every person actually exists in an existential situation that includes a real subjective possibility of reaching a supernatural goal by accepting God's self-donation in grace.[29] It was mentioned earlier that the "actual grace" impelling human existence to salvation, which consists in accepting in faith and love God's free and personal gift of himself, is the supernatural existential itself. Moreover, this is to be understood in terms of concrete experiences of the impulse to self-transcendence. Actually, the consciousness of all persons is so altered that they are open to God (implicitly, however, and not as to an object known) through the "dynamism of the spirit's transcendence into the infinity of the silent mystery which we call God."[30] God thus offers himself to and is present to the conscious experience of every person. If people *accept* the supernaturally graced impulses of their own transcendent and spiritual nature, they have in effect accepted a real revelation from God and have made an act of faith, however implicit and anonymous it may be.[31]

Translating this into the terms of the boundary experiences described above, it can be said that every person is actually exposed to God's "divine, supernatural grace which offers an interior union with God and by means of which God communicates himself whether the individual takes up an attitude of acceptance or refusal towards this grace."[32] It follows that "wherever, and in so far as, the individual makes a moral decision in this life, . . . this moral decision can also be thought to measure up to the character of a supernaturally elevated, believing and thus saving act."[33] In this way Rahner sees God's justifying and saving grace, that is, his personal gift of himself, being accepted by an implicit act of faith and love outside Christianity. And one might presume, precisely because of the universality and the efficacy of God's salvific will, that the vast majority of people are actually saved in this way. "Theology has been too long and too often bedevilled by the unavowed supposition that grace would no longer be grace if it were too generously distributed by the love of God!"[34] This position has implications for our understanding of human history.

Grace and History

Because of the unity of nature and grace, and that from the very beginning, there is a material identity and coextensiveness between the history of this world and the history of salvation. The so-called profane history of the world is the history of salvation and grace. In stating this, however, Rahner makes some careful distinctions and qualifications.

First of all there is a distinction between "profane" history and the history of salvation because ultimately salvation is the secret of an internal and personal decision. Salvation is a function of a free faith decision and the saving or damning character of freedom cannot be known objectively. Therefore the general history of salvation is not strictly historical in the sense of being objectified and public. It cannot be known in an explicit and definitive way that salvation is indeed going on in it.[35] Nor should it be thought that salvation (or grace) is generated by history alone, that it is achieved by the actions of human beings in history: Salvation is always a pure gift of grace.[36]

Rahner thus preserves the same distinction between world history and salvation history as between nature and grace in order to show that the history of the world is other than and different from grace. It is precisely to this autonomous history that God addresses his personal love, grace and salvation.[37]

But after these distinctions are made, because the salvific will of God concretizes itself in the world, in the actual situation and life of every person, all of profane history is really the history of salvation. Profane history and salvation history are unified; they are one. Moreover, this history is a history of revelation because grace manifests itself in consciousness and awareness and is accepted in faith, at least anonymously.[38]

It might be good to sum up what has been said so far in terms of general principles. What is the relation between grace and nature, between the order of redemption and the order of creation, between the supernatural order and the natural order? They are not simply identical according to Rahner, but are distinct. The created or natural order of the world and history is as it were a relatively autonomous realm that is one in itself. And yet the whole purpose of the created world and its history is redemption; there is only one creative intention in the Creator and this intention is to redeem and to save by communicating himself supernaturally to what he created. The whole creative purpose, then, is governed by the supernatural and redemptive purpose of God. The natural or created order is thus related to the order of grace, redemption and the supernatural self-donation of God to it as a necessary presupposition for this free gift. In terms of the principle of unity and distinction, the natural and supernatural orders are radically distinct; they are the effects of two, as it were, different actions of God *ad extra*. God communicates himself to what he already sustains in existence. But the two are also radically one and coextensive because of the design of God. Thus Rahner says:

> In the concrete order of supernatural divine self-communication as in fact willed by God, every natural created entity is ordered to this grace in such a way that it cannot remain really whole and healthy in itself, nor achieve the completion required by its own nature, except as integrated into the supernatural order of

grace. In the concrete order, then, nature itself can find its way to its own completion only if it realizes that it is actually a factor within the all-embracing reality of grace and redemption.[39]

The Validity of Other Religions

Approaching other religions from a strictly theological point of view, and again basing his position on the supernatural existential, Rahner explains why other religions can be considered supernatural, lawful and positively willed by God in terms of Christianity itself.

On the one hand, from the point of view of the operation of grace, while on the whole the gift of salvation in grace lies hidden in world history at large, still that does not mean that it remains completely private and secret and hidden in individual consciences. No, grace becomes manifest in human lives and it breaks forth through objective and public signs, in the lives of actual people and through them in institutions. Outside Christianity and outside Old Testament religion before it, supernatural grace "will make itself felt in the concrete history of man." It will become manifest in actual religious forms and structures. In this way it is not difficult to see how religions outside the Christian tradition can be seen as "quite legitimate in the saving providence of God" and at the same time supernatural and positively willed by him.[40]

On the other hand, from the point of view of how a person comes in contact with grace, non-Christian religions again appear as lawful, supernatural and willed by God. For every person in all situations of history must have an actually effective and concrete possibility of salvation. But because of the social nature of human existence and the social nature of religion, this real possibility of grace cannot be had outside of the concrete religious institutions in which any given person lives his or her life. Therefore, in fact, the positive and salvific relationship of a person to God will be had "within *that* religion which [is] at his disposal by being a factor in his sphere of existence."[41] Because grace can come to people only through the concrete world of their actual historical period and will come through the social forms of their religion, Rahner concludes:

> The religions existing in the concrete must contain supernatural, gratuitous elements, and in using *these* elements the pre-Christian was able to attain God's grace: presumably, too, the pre-Christian exists even to this day, even though the possibility is gradually disappearing *today*.[42]

On both these accounts, then, other non-Christian religions can be considered valid in the sense of supernatural and positively willed by God in his plan of salvation for humankind, even though not in all their aspects. Rahner uses the analogy of their being related to Christianity as Old Covenant religion is to Christianity, with the significant difference, however, that in the latter case Christianity issued out of the Jewish religious tradition. But on the same analogy and for the same reasons that Rahner gives, one can see how basic religious traditions and institutions of other religions might be preserved within Christianity, how their Scriptures might be considered truly graced and inspired, and the revelation they contain used in Christian liturgy.

Anonymous Christianity

The implications of the lawfulness of other religions because of the presence of a supernatural experience of grace that may underlie them is drawn out by Rahner in Christian terms under the name "anonymous Christianity." It is most important that one see the logic of this term: It is a Christian word, which defines first of all a Christian self-understanding vis-à-vis the continuing pluralism of religions. It represents an attempt to understand the world and other religions in terms of the definitive character of *Christ's* grace. It is *not* a term to be addressed to non-Christians; it is a term applicable to others when Christians talk about them in terms of the revelation of grace we have received in Jesus Christ. From many other points of view the term may seem unacceptable, but this will not concern us here.

The term "anonymously Christian" can be applied on two lev-

els, to persons and to religious institutions. In both cases, the supernatural existential appears as the fundamental premise of Rahner's
statements. Grace is universally offered to people through the transcendence and the occasions for self-transcendence of their spiritual
nature. Acceptance of the transcendent aspect of human existence is
itself a movement of and an acceptance of grace, and it implies a new
conscious awareness that can be called a revelation and an implicit
faith. Thus, if the non-Christian.

> has experienced the grace of God—if, in certain circumstances,
> he has already accepted this grace as the ultimate, unfathomable
> entelechy of his existence by accepting the immeasurableness of
> his dying existence as opening out into infinity—then he has
> already been given revelation in a true sense even before he has
> been affected by missionary preaching from without. For this
> grace understood as the *a priori* horizon of all his spiritual acts,
> accompanies his consciousness subjectively, even though it is
> not known objectively. And the revelation which comes to him
> from without is not in such a case the proclamation of some-
> thing as yet absolutely unknown. . . . Such a revelation is then
> the expression in objective concepts of something which this
> person has already attained or could already have attained in
> the depth of his rational existence.[43]

On the level of institutional religion, then, Rahner says that it is
"absolutely permissible for the Christian himself to interpret this
non-Christianity as Christianity of an anonymous kind."[44] The
Church is thus not to be seen as the exclusive community of grace
and salvation. Rather it is "the historically tangible vanguard and
the historically and socially constituted explicit expression of what
the Christian hopes is present as a hidden reality even outside the
visible Church."[45] Christianity therefore is not opposed to other religions as to those who lack grace, revelation or salvation. Rather the
opposition should be set on the axis of implicit and explicit knowledge of the source of this gift. This does not mean that the natural
development of non-Christian religions toward Christianity, at least
theoretically speaking, is not to be desired. After all, anonymity is a
very ambiguous state.

Christianity and Profane History

In dealing with Christianity and the world, Christian salvation and profane history, Rahner's views display a severe tension or polarity between two almost opposing attitudes. On the one hand, the ultimate salvation of humankind cannot be thought of as occurring in this world. Ultimate salvation is the cessation of the history of this world and it occurs in eternity and out of this world. Moreover, it will be effected for the individual and the race by God and not by humanity itself; it is not in the power of human existence. And for this reason, the Christian view of salvation demythologizes and relativizes the world and its history. Christianity underlines the fact that neither the world nor anything in it is God, that history and the world are subject to human control to some extent, but that salvation must come from a different source. Thus Christian faith involves a radical skepticism about the possible achievements of humankind in this world; salvation is an eschatological reality on the other side of history. In the Christian vision, world history is thus devalued in relation to ultimate and eternal salvation.[46]

On the other hand, salvation takes place in this world and the history of this world is the history of salvation. Christianity enhances the world's value and takes history seriously precisely because it is the finite field where salvation begins and is worked out. In this sense, the world and profane history are absolutized because in the Christian view they exist as a creation that is ordained toward God's love and salvation.[47]

It is absolutely necessary to see the tension here if one is to appreciate what Rahner says about the Christian life of grace in this world. On the one hand, ultimate salvation comes to its completion in eternity, and one is in contact with the eternal love of God in grace. On the other, humanity exists in this world, grace approaches us only here, and we must work out our salvation in fear and trembling. Depending on the focus one chooses, the world and human history can appear devalued and relativized in relation to ultimate salvation, or it can take on a new and absolute importance as that which will be saved and as the where of the accomplishment of this destiny. These same two poles ought to be reflected, then, in the Christian life.

The Christian Life of Grace in the World

In describing Christian experience and Christian life of grace in this world, Rahner alternates between Christians' freedom from the world and their concern for the world and its this-worldly future. He points alternately to what can be described as a vertical and a horizontal dimension in the Christian experience of grace and its consequent concern.

In the experience of grace, Christians are in touch with eternity in their transcendent acts of freedom. And in that experience they experience as well the essential finitude of everything in this world and of every future in it. This finitude and limitedness is manifested on every level; the limitedness and finitude of this world is seen in temporality itself, a temporality whose outer and definitive sign is death.[48] But in Christ's grace, Christians have already overcome this finitude and participate now in God's infinity and absoluteness, and they will find their ultimate and absolute future there. In knowing the absolute meaning of human life and destiny, and in being already in contact with and in a sense in possession of this salvation, Christians ought to regard every plan and project for the future of this world in this world as not worthy of an absolute concern.[49]

On the other hand, however, the Christian's faith in and experience of an absolute future includes and grounds the importance of the future of this world. Christians know that this world, even in its materiality, will participate in the full and "glorified" achievement of the human spirit. Christians realize that they are in the world and cannot withdraw from it. And they can, to a certain extent, be obliged to cooperate in the creation of new this-worldly structures and to work for the progress of the race.[50] But this is not a concern of the Church, Rahner adds. Historical affairs are relatively autonomous and the Church as such has no clear blueprint for the future. In speaking of the Church's progress Rahner describes it somewhat introspectively in terms of its own inner life; but it must adapt itself to the exigencies of contemporary history.[51]

Critical Observations

It should be remembered that the discussion of the Christian's and the Church's involvement in the world has advanced considerably since Rahner wrote these articles. And he himself has had more to say on the matter. But his statement in these articles at least may be questioned. In the concluding chapter we shall see some of Rahner's post–Vatican II contributions to the role of the Church in history.

To summarize the problem, it may be said that the Christian understanding of history and the world does contain an unmediated dialectic of two almost opposing forces and ideas that can lead to conflicting attitudes and spiritualities. This is seen in Christian eschatology where salvation is described as "already" and as "not yet"; already, because the Christian has been established in a vertical relationship to God and experiences himself caught up in this eternal love; not yet, because one still has his or her life to live in this world. We Christians must live with others in this world; we still have sin and its effects to reckon with; the absolute future thus remains obscure for us and we must advance toward it relying on God's grace and not our own power. The problem is seen for the Church when it is described as in the world and yet not of it. Any emphasis on human desire and concern for building a better world might appear as Pelagian, idealistic and forgetful that salvation is the work of God alone; it might distract from the religious experience of God's *grace* and of the transcendent character of this *gift* of fulfillment and salvation. But an emphasis on the other-worldly and eternal aspect of salvation in which one already participates could minimize human responsibility to others and for the world in which people actually suffer from the effects of sin.

In his salvation history articles Rahner continually moves back and forth between the terms of this dialectic. Perhaps because he is dialoguing with Marxism, however, he remains too much an existentialist in terms of *personal* union with God in the present moment, and not enough concerned with the future of this world. The relationship between the two attitudes of the dialectic do not have to be left hanging as a "both/and." At least they can be seen as more positively interrelated. Here Luther's insight into the possible effects of grace takes on its full meaning. The Christian's freedom *from* the world and history is precisely a freedom *for* the world and its history; it is a freedom for a service to the neighbor. Precisely because salvation is "right now," the Christian is liberated into a service of gratitude and is liberated to love others for their own sake. In terms of the Church, the community of Christians, even as a public institution and sign of salvation and grace, may then be seen as an institution that is not introspective or in service of itself but in service to the world. The visible manifestation of grace will become all the more tangible to the extent that the community of Christians serve others concretely in this world.

There can be no doubt that this is a very idealistic vision of things. But it may still be the mark of what a Christian attitude should be. If the Christian views the world and its history as precisely salvation history because God is at work in it through his grace, then, faced with the fundamental option between pessimism (for which there are apparently real reasons and motives) and optimism (for which there are also real motives) regarding the future of *this world*, a final Christian realism should not lead toward dark suspicion but toward hope and commitment.

Conclusion

A summary and concluding appreciation of Rahner is particularly difficult precisely because he is so close to us. Distance is needed for appreciation, and history has its own peculiar and erratic way of judging a thinker according to the consequences of his thought. It is difficult, too, because in a period of upheaval in Catholic theology Rahner appears as a transitional figure, but one who has constructed a theology of immense stature and proportion. He is old and he is new; he is radically critical of Scholasticism, while at the same time he is very dependent on it as well as very reverent and cautious regarding tradition in general. A testimony to the greatness of Rahner, however, is the way many of his ideas are simply presumed by common Catholic consciousness today. And these ideas were fashioned in a period when ordinary Catholic theology was moribund, and in a period when the conservative and frightened reaction to Modernism was still in the air. If the context for understanding grace today is no longer that of Scholasticism, and if Catholic theology is enjoying a new freedom and renaissance, this is largely due to certain theologians of the thirties, forties and fifties, and among them Rahner is probably *the* leading figure.

Rahner's contribution to a theology of grace is massive. Perhaps, in conclusion, two of his most important theological interpretations can be simply recalled. First of all, Rahner is one of the major figures bridging an ontological understanding of grace, as in Scholasticism, and an understanding of grace in personalist terms of encounter. And in his thought, that bridge itself still remains, for grace is basically God's personal self-communication to persons by quasi-formal causality. Many maintain that one cannot adequately speak of grace without at some point resorting to ontological language. As Rahner himself says, if the effects of grace are real, they should be able to be described in the categories of being. It still remains to be seen whether or not a full account of grace can be achieved in phenomenological and personalist categories.[52]

Second, Rahner has to a large extent helped to overcome the dualism between the natural and supernatural orders and the consequent extrinsicism of previous understandings of grace. In Rahner's language of grace the natural and the supernatural orders are radically one. It must have been noted that Rahner still retains the word supernatural in spite of the contemporary dysfunctionality of this word. Although the word should certainly be dropped because it is not necessary to express Rahner's concerns, those concerns themselves are valid. For Rahner the word serves to emphasize the distinction between the two orders, the gift quality or gratuitousness of grace and salvation, and the fact that God remains radically transcendent in relation to humanity. Moreover, the distinction underlines the fact that the Christian vision is the very opposite of pantheism; God has created human beings other than himself and he enters into a new supernatural relation of dialogue with them through his grace. But still the natural and the supernatural orders are one and coterminous. People experience grace in their lives in this world; they experience grace in the concrete situations of daily life and the concerns that make up the occasions of limit and self-transcendence. The history of grace and salvation and the history of this world are one. And from this many other things follow.

Notes

1. Karl Rahner, *Spirit in the World*, trans. William Dych (New York: Herder and Herder, 1968). Cf. pp. xlix–lv for Rahner's statement of his method, that is, how he interprets Aquinas. The basic bio-data presented here can be found in Herbert Vorgrimler, *Karl Rahner: His Life, Thought and Works*, trans. Edward Quinn (Glen Rock, N.J.: Paulist Press, 1965).

2. Karl Rahner, *Hearers of the Word*, trans. Michael Richards (New York: Herder and Herder, 1969).

3. A systematic account of grace by Rahner can be found in *Sacramentum Mundi* II (New York: Herder and Herder, 1968), pp. 415–422.

4. A very technical account of this principle can be seen in Rahner's article "The Theology of Symbol," *Theological Investigations* IV (Baltimore: Helicon Press, 1966), pp. 221–252, passim. A brief statement in less technical terms can be found in "The Order of Redemption within the Order of Creation," in *The Christian Commitment*, trans. Cecily Hastings (New York: Sheed and Ward, 1963), pp. 44–46. Important philosophical background for the concept of reciprocal causality is found in Rahner's treatment of "Conversion to the Phantasm," *Spirit in the World*, pp. 237–383, and in his essay *Hominisation*, trans. W. T. O'Hara (New York: Herder and Herder, 1965), pp. 45–101.

5. The article is found in *Theological Investigations* I (Baltimore: Helicon Press, 1961), pp. 319–346 (cited hereafter as "Implications").

6. Peter Fransen, *The New Life of Grace* (Tournai: Desclee & Company, 1969), pp. 94–95.

7. Rahner, "Implications," pp. 320–325.

8. Ibid., pp. 325–326.

9. Ibid., p. 327.

10. The category and term "quasi-formal causality" should not be allowed to distract one from Rahner's point. The term is derived from Aristotle's theory of hylomorphism, that is, the theory of matter and form, material causality and formal causality. Rahner speaks of "quasi" formal causality because it is predicated of God and therefore only analogically. It is distinguished from "efficient causality" by which God creates and sustains all being. God's quasi-formal causality is, as it were, a second action of God in relation to the creature, the basis of a new supernatural relation with human existence. The idea of a form and formal causality represents here an "active being present to"; "informing" is causing by being actively there. In the *visio*, the idea might be expressed as God's flooding human spiritual being and consciousness with his presence.

11. Rahner, "Implications," pp. 334–335.

12. Ibid., p. 336. Rahner writes in another place: "Grace is God himself, the communication in which he gives himself to man as the divinizing favour which he is himself. Here his work is really *himself*, since it is he who is imparted. Such grace, from the very start, cannot be thought of independently of the personal love of God and its answer in man." He then adds that

because this interpersonal relationship is real and has real effects, it should not exclude ontological language. But such categories should not be misunderstood; they do *not* exhaust the reality of grace and should not be allowed to distort its meaning ("Nature and Grace," *Theological Investigations* IV [Baltimore: Helicon Press, 1966], p. 177. Cf. also p. 175).

13. Rahner, "Nature and Grace," p. 176.

14. Cf. *supra*, pp. 72–73.

15. *Theological Investigations* I, pp. 297–317 (cited hereafter as "Relationship").

16. Rahner, "Relationship," pp. 298–300. An extended, most comprehensive and conclusive critique of extrinsicism was given by Blondel and Laberthonnière and Le Roy during the Modernist period in France. Blondel coined the term for Catholic theology. It should be added that while Rahner's "supernatural existential" is original and his own, very similar ideas were proposed by Laberthonnière and Blondel at the turn of the century.

17. Cf. ibid., pp. 303–306. We prescind here from whether or not Rahner's presentation of the position of the *nouvelle théologie* is correct and especially from whether his criticism is accurate. Similar criticisms were made of Blondel, who to some extent inspired the *nouvelle théologie*, and these are not accurate.

18. Ibid., pp. 302–303.

19. In his *Theological Dictionary* Rahner describes the supernatural existential as the dogmatic fact that our concrete, actual historical state is one of being called to grace, which means that "antecedently to justification by grace, received sacramentally or extra-sacramentally, man is already subject to the universal salvific will of God, he *is* already redeemed and absolutely obliged to tend to his supernatural end. This 'situation' is not merely an external one; it is an objective, ontological qualification of man, added indeed to his nature by God's grace and therefore supernatural, but in fact never lacking in the real order" (Karl Rahner and Herbert Vorgrimler, *Theological Dictionary* [New York: Herder and Herder, 1965], p. 161).

20. If a desire or natural necessity for grace were of nature as such, the gratuity of grace would be undermined. For grace to appear as given *freely* by God, as unexacted and unowed to human existence, the orientation to it in a created nature must also be considered a gift (Rahner, "Relationship," pp. 312–313).

21. Ibid., pp. 313–315. In fact, however, one can never tell what in positive human experience is of nature and what of grace.

22. Cf. Rahner, "Nature and Grace," pp. 176–177, for an indication of this.

23. This question is also treated in Rahner's article "Nature and Grace," pp. 165–168, and in the short "Reflections on the Experience of Grace," *Theological Investigations* III (Baltimore: Helicon Press, 1967), pp. 86–90.

24. Rahner, "Relationship," pp. 298–299.

25. Rahner, "Nature and Grace," pp. 166–168.

26. Ibid., p. 183.

27. Ibid., pp. 178–179.

28. Ibid., pp. 183–184. Cf. also "Reflections on the Experience of Grace," pp. 86–90, where Rahner describes further the kinds of experiences in which grace is especially operative and conscious.

29. Rahner, "History of the World and Salvation-History," *Theological Investigations* V (Baltimore: Helicon Press, 1966), p. 103 (cited hereafter as "Salvation History").

30. Rahner, "Salvation History," p. 104.

31. Ibid., p. 104. It should be noted that while the supernatural existential is truly a supernaturally elevated mode of existence and in that sense grace and a gift, it is not justifying grace. For justifying grace needs an acceptance of God in a free act of faith and love (Rahner, "Nature and Grace," p.179). The supernatural existential is a "deficient mode of grace," an orientation to and an offer of God's self-communication, but is "not simply the same grace as the divine self-communication itself" (Karl Rahner, "Questions of Controversial Theology on Justification," *Theological Investigations* IV, pp. 200, 215–217).

32. Karl Rahner, "Christianity and the Non-Christian Religions," *Theological Investigations* V, p. 123 (cited hereafter as "Non-Christian Religions").

33. Rahner, "Non-Christian Religions," p. 125. Rahner writes in another place: "In a case, for instance, where the natural moral law is *de facto* being observed, the healing grace of God is *de facto* being given even if the person concerned does not know it and has not expressly desired it. But we Christians, at least, ought to be aware of this openness within all natural things directing them towards the ordering of grace. We ought not merely to be stating it as a theoretical fact, here and there, once in a while; we ought to be experiencing it more and more, in the concrete, in everyday life, and putting it into detailed practice. We need to be gradually waking up to the fact that the detailed events and actions of concrete human existence are always in fact, even in their very naturalness, something more than merely natural" ("The Order of Redemption within the Order of Creation," p. 51).

34. Rahner, "Nature and Grace," p. 180.

35. Rahner, "Salvation History," pp. 100–102. For this reason Rahner distinguishes general salvation history from salvation history strictly so-called, in which the grace of God is manifested tangibly, objectively and unambiguously in the Incarnation of Christ and the history of Christianity. There the history of salvation becomes public in the visible Church, "objectively" known and therefore strictly historical (ibid., pp. 106–109). This paradoxical situation of grace and redemption being simultaneously hidden and manifest in world history stems precisely from grace's being imbedded in nature and world history. This is true even after Christ. Thus Rahner writes: "The order of redemption, as a whole, is in the first place an object of faith; despite the fact that the redemptive order does manifest itself in won-

ders and signs of the power of the Spirit, faith must affirm it as not simply accessible to experience and hence as something hidden. The unity is further hidden in that God's grace, with its power to save the world, works for the most part anonymously and can itself be mistaken for one of the forces and potentialities inherent in the world. . . . In other words: The redemptive order itself is hidden in the darkness of faith, its power over the world is always subject to misinterpretation as a power immanent in the world, and furthermore never seems, even when it is recognized as divine power, to achieve anything final in the world but seems subject to the world's own stronger law, the law of dissolution and death. The unity of the created and redemptive orders is hidden, and its very hiddenness represents a danger to its fulfilment" ("The Order of Redemption within the Order of Creation," pp. 59–60).

36. Rahner, "Salvation History," pp. 100–102.

37. Ibid., p. 114.

38. Ibid., pp. 102-105. Rahner develops the connection of revelation to grace in "Observations on the Concept of Revelation," in Rahner and Joseph Ratzinger, *Revelation and Tradition* (New York: Herder and Herder, 1966), pp. 9–25.

39. Rahner, "The Order of Redemption within the Order of Creation," p. 50. Cf. also pp. 41–53. "God has not created two realities needing subsequently to be, so to speak, harmonized. Rather, he has constituted the whole of reality distinct from himself, to which he communicates himself, according to one ultimate, primordial intention, so that it all has a primordial unity and every difference in it springs from that unity as a mode of the unity itself, the unity preceding the differences which arise from it and which must precisely for its sake be respected. So if we want to formulate the relation of the supernatural to the natural order, we can equally well speak of the redemptive order within the created order or of the created order within the redemptive order" (Ibid., p. 52).

40. Rahner, "Salvation History," pp. 197–198, 202–203.

41. Rahner, "Non-Christian Religions," p. 128.

42. Ibid., p. 130.

43. Ibid., p. 131.

44. Ibid., p. 133.

45. Ibid.

46. Rahner, "Salvation History," pp. 97–98, 110–113.

47. Ibid., pp. 112–114.

48. Rahner, "Christianity and the 'New Man,'" *Theological Investigations* V, pp. 140–143.

49. Ibid., pp. 146–147.

50. Ibid., pp. 146–149.

51. Ibid., pp. 151–152.

52. Cf. Francis Colborn, "The Theology of Grace: Present Trends and Future Directions," *Theological Studies* 31 (December 1970): 692–711.

7

Liberation: A Contemporary Language of Graced Experience

Our study of grace has been an essay of historical theology. As historical, it has been an attempt to understand how other past figures have understood that which we Christians experience and call "grace." There can be no doubt that Augustine, Aquinas, Luther, Trent and even Rahner have helped determine for us the meaning of the word grace. The content of Christian faith comes from a historical past and there can be no adequate understanding of the doctrine of grace without an understanding of the origins of that doctrine in the people who first formulated it. As theological, however, our study of the past has transcended "mere history." The thought-world of any past figure is conditioned by suppositions of a historical period that are no longer ours. In trying to understand the meaning of grace itself through the thought of others, one has to examine the context of statements, uncover suppositions, look at the method and logic of thinking, lay bare special biases, and judge conclusions in the light of and in relation to our present situation and experience of the matter. Theology is thus critical understanding and it involves making judgments on the object of faith that is present to our faith experience right now.

The educational value of historical theology is largely experimental.[1] That is to say, the main fruit of the study is not objective knowledge that one acquires of the past, nor even the objective content concerning the object of study, which in this case is grace. These of course are not to be minimized. But far more important is an insight into what might be called the theological process itself. The close study of different representative authors of different periods can mediate a personal understanding of how theological understanding itself is historically conditioned and why different understandings not only are, but must be, generated in different cultures. The investigations of historical theology thus lead to a truly paradoxical consequence: The more we critically appreciate the past, on which we are really dependent, the more we are liberated from that past and able to create new forms of understanding. In more concrete terms: The more one realizes the extent to which common tradition was once really indigenous to another culture, context and personal experience, the more one will realize *why* contemporary indigenization is possible, *why* it is necessary, and *how* and *to what extent* it can be effected.

But besides stimulating personal and reflective understanding, this essay in historical theology has also uncovered a good deal of content concerning the doctrine of grace. In this chapter we shall summarize and draw together the various theologies of grace that have been presented in the preceding chapters. After considering the dialectic between experience and understanding, between experience and language, in brief successive interpretative surveys, ever widening in their focus, we shall consider the shifting problematics, the nature and the effects of grace as they appear in the history of the theology of grace. We shall conclude with a consideration of the Christian life under grace experienced as a liberating force in human life. In the final chapter of the book we shall use all this data for constructing a view of history under the influence of God's grace.

The Christian Experience and Language of Grace

Rahner has established theologically in terms of Catholic theology what William James presupposed fifty years before, namely, that the action of God in human life can be experienced.[2] Grace, that is, God's ordination of human existence to a personal union with himself and his offer of the gift of himself, is an integral part of actual human nature. This means that grace is an indistinguishable element not only of human being, but also of the deepest movements in a person's spirit, consciousness and even in some cases psychology.[3] An appreciation of the operation of grace in this world requires, perhaps, an analytic or philosophical recognition of human transcendence, but it can also be seen in a descriptive account of how this is played out in conscious religious experience. Concretely, it is on this second level alone, and not on the level of theology, that the problems connected with the doctrine of grace can be met and solved.

The problems involved in any doctrine of grace are both theoretical and concrete. Reductively they can all be reduced to the problem of evil, to the negative or dark side of human existence. The existence and experience of evil in the world—the physical evil of sickness, disease and death and the moral evil of sin and its inescapable effects—is a permanent and internal threat to the doctrine of God's love. The theme of evil is the background not only in Augustine and Luther's theology of grace; it is the permanent background of every theology of grace. In some cases the experience of evil can totally blind a person to a recognition of God's graciousness; in others, the doctrine of grace may be accepted but with the question mark of serious doubt. Evil is experienced by every person, personally and concretely in his or her own life. It is not therefore a distant problem. Without an appreciation of this persistent and dialectical element in human experience, there is a danger that an understanding of and one's talk about grace will be superficial and facile. But if this dialectical element is kept in mind, one has a better chance of meeting experience realistically, understanding it and communicating it to people according to their situations.

Ultimately and concretely, the problems connected with the doctrine of grace find their solution in the experience of grace itself. The Christian apologist who wants to explain and communicate what can be known of God's love will have to point to the human experiences in which it is found and the signs in which it is manifest. Ultimately, he or she will point to Christ, who is the definitive revealer of God's love and who *is* God's grace, and to his Spirit, which has been poured out in the hearts of his followers and is operative in all of history. But to do this with conviction and credibility it helps to know *how* that grace of Christ is experienced.

The intention here is not to reanalyze the varieties of the experience of grace or to summarize *all* possible religious experiences. But what should be pointed out as one looks back over the history of the theology of grace is the significance of these experiences and their diversity. First of all, for grace to be real, it must be experienced in some way. And grace *is* real because it is operative concretely and subjectively in people and it manifests itself in their lives. It appears in various forms because it works in persons with different personalities, temperaments, backgrounds, and so on. Second, then, the working of grace in concrete natures means quite simply that it is to be expected that there will be a great variety of ways in which individuals experience God's grace. Thus, on the one hand, one can say that behind every doctrine of grace there is some religious experience. There is no doctrine of grace that does not entail and, indeed, rest on some experience of transcendence. An understanding of any doctrine of grace thus implies a grasp of that experience in some form or other. And on the other hand, for different experiences of grace there will be different nuances of doctrine. One can expect a certain pluralism in doctrines that try to express the richness of God's love.

Basic Problems

The legacy of Augustine to the theology of grace is a conception that finally came to sharp focus in his prolonged controversy with Pelagius or with what he understood to be Pelagianism. Grace is understood in the context of and relative to human freedom and love. In Augustine's thought grace is closely identified with the immanent working of the Spirit of God within the human personality and consequently within history. For the profoundly questioning mind of Augustine, grace alone responds to the question of the ultimate source of human goodness, to the question: Why is there human goodness at all in the world? Ultimately, he says, it is God's grace that is responsible for self-transcending love and the consequent expanding of the horizon of freedom beyond mere choice of objects or decisions based on self-centered designs. This understanding has been written into the doctrine of the Church. For his part Augustine did not extend the working of grace universally beyond the Christian order of things. But it follows from the Augustinian doctrine that where there is authentic self-transcending love, there God's saving grace is operative.[4]

During the course of the thirteenth century and through the

assumption of the categories of Aristotle's philosophy of nature, the context for understanding grace radically shifted. The climax of this development is seen in Aquinas's later treatment of grace in his *Summa Theologiae*. Although the central Augustinian assertions remain, Aquinas's understanding of grace is at bottom fundamentally different. In his thought grace is seen relative to the human person and race as finite and limited, as created "nature." In this context grace is a new power and nature, elevating and supernatural, and also divinizing because through this habitual gift to the soul one "participates" in God's own life. Grace is absolutely and metaphysically necessary for attaining eternal salvation because the finite created nature is teleologically incapable of reaching the supernatural and revealed goal of communion with God to which we are called. Human beings, then, precisely as human beings, are transformed and raised up by the infusion of a new quality and level of being called grace.

Although such themes as the absolute transcendence and sovereignty of God carry over from the *via moderna* into the reformers, still the development in Luther's theology of grace is really a sharp break with the Scholastic mode of thought. Here the understanding of grace is set in the context of an interpersonal relationship between God and the human person with the Word as the mediator. Grace is defined relative to human sinfulness: God's grace is forgiving. Although this theme is common to both Augustine and Aquinas, it is central to Luther and explained by him in considerably different fashion. Grace is God's mercy, forgiveness and love for the sinner as a person, and in and through this personal relationship, sustained by the Word and an actual faith response, the sinner is transformed even while concupiscence or sin remains.

Much of Rahner's earliest theology of grace, while it retains an absolutely fundamental position in his thought, is directed to overcoming the problems that had become inherent in the Scholastic language of grace. Starting from Scholastic premises, he argues to the primacy of uncreated grace and thereby overcomes the objectivist view of Scholastic categories by justifying personalist categories for talk about grace. Second, arguing against extrinsicism he establishes the unity of the natural and supernatural orders and thus overcomes the dualism implicit in the then current neo-Scholasticism with his concept of the "supernatural existential." The real advance in the theology of grace mediated by Rahner then occurs when he views grace in the context of universal human history and eschatology. God's salvific will is universal, and grace is God's personal offer and presence of himself to all people across the whole of history. While all the major themes of the past are preserved in Rahner's understanding, there is a decided shift and development here, for grace is seen as operating generally and universally outside the boundaries of Christianity, in a concrete existential way as well as in a public and social way in other religions.

Here then are four fundamental aspects and themes, all of which, except the last, are in a sometimes more, sometimes less, degree common to the history of the Christian understanding of grace. Grace is God's love for human beings, a love that affects, converts and transforms human freedom and loving, a love that is accepting and forgiving, a love that raises a person up to become a "new kind of existence"; and, it may be added, since this love is universally offered to and operative in all human beings, it is at work transforming history.

Grace Itself

From the very beginning the word grace in the Christian vocabulary has stood for the favor and love that God bestows upon humanity in Christ and in the Christian dispensation. The word emphasizes the qualities of that love of God for human beings; it is totally gratuitous, offered to us in complete freedom on God's part. And in this sense everything that God does for humanity in Christ is grace. From this point of view, the word grace has almost no precise content that is distinct from the whole mystery of Christ's revelation and redemption and the gift of his Spirit, in short, the whole Christian economy. It is important to realize that the word can never really be divorced from this very broad context. The study of every aspect of Christian doctrine is thus a study of grace.

Grace, then, refers to the relationship of love that God has established with humanity, and that is revealed in Jesus Christ. The word "grace" stands for *how*, in the Christian experience, God relates to human beings, how he deals with people, and how consequently we stand in relation to God. More and more, especially beginning with Augustine in the West, how human existence stands in relationship with God and how God deals with us began to be understood in the context of specific problems. Thus the history of the theology and doctrine of grace also became somewhat specialized; it deals with humanity's concrete, here-and-now relation with God in the Christian dispensation, that is, in Christ. But this involves the most general and basic views of what humanity is, of Christian anthropology, and of how God addresses humankind in this world and in history. These have become the fundamental issues in the doctrine of grace. From a certain point of view, then, the question of grace is absolutely fundamental, and the answers to these questions will determine one's understanding of the very meaning of Christian life and Christian spirituality.

The word "language" as used in the title of this study, however, concerns much more than the question of vocabulary and the meaning of a word. The idea of language has been employed here analogously to mean a whole system and logic for understanding. Such a system of understanding is determined by its historical context, by the cultural forces at work, by the specific problems encountered and addressed, by the sources of human thought that one borrows to address them, by the personal experience of the user of these sources. For this reason there are diverse languages of grace, that is, diverse ways of understanding it.

Augustine addresses the question of grace in the context of our sin, our freedom and unfreedom to do good, and our ability and inability to accept the salvation that God offers us in his election and love. Grace for Augustine is primarily a force in the inner life of a person calling to faith and assisting the will to do good. Grace becomes the Spirit, the Spirit of love, that turns *cupiditas* into *caritas*, liberates a person from selfishness and gives him or her the very power to love God and what is good. Without this healing grace we are hopelessly prisoners of a will twisted by sin, and this remains a permanent obstacle to our salvation, that is, the final union with and possession of God for which we are ordained. But with grace God quietly, but sometimes with great spiritual turmoil, draws those chosen by his love back to himself. For the first time in the history of Christian thought, Augustine clearly asserts that the power of salvation, God's grace, works internally and directly within the human will.

In Aquinas grace is seen in a cosmological framework. Grace is a new form of being; it is a supernatural nature that God in his love bestows on the Christian, on one who responds to his revelation in loving faith, and so raises him up. This new form of being elevates a person and gives one a participation above nature in the divine life itself. And as a principle of human actions, grace enables a person to act on a supernatural level, proportionate to one's calling. By grace we are sanctified and enabled to live a life that is worthy of salvation, that is, final spiritual union with God. In Aquinas, grace is primarily the created effect of God's working within us; it is a new form of being.

In Luther grace is God's word and promise of mercy and forgiveness. As in Augustine, grace is set in the context of sin, but sin now has a significantly different and more comprehensive meaning. Sin has much more to do with a person's being and fundamental worth than with one's actions. In spite of sin, however, God addresses us personally in Christ and guarantees that we are forgiven, acceptable and saved. And this personal relationship of real forgiveness transforms the Christian and allows him or her to live a completely new life of freedom. Grace in Luther is basically external to human existence but assimilated and appropriated by an interpersonal relationship to God in Christ.

In Trent, too, grace is forgiveness, as well as much more. Grace is primarily an inner renovation of the human person, giving one a new birth into a new form of life. Grace is a new state of being, given by God and inhering in us so that it becomes our own. It is a participation in Christ's grace, that is to say, God's love incarnate.

In Rahner, grace is most fundamentally God's gift of his very self to human persons in love. This gift is offered to every person at every period of history, and this permanent offer of himself is itself a completely gratuitous decision on God's part, one that raises the world and its history into a supernatural state of existence. While humans are dependent on God for their being, still they are created distinct from God with an autonomy that allows them to freely respond to God's love. The whole of history, then, is a dialogue in which God addresses persons in love and people respond to this offer of God's self-donation as it is manifesed in their lives and experience. This offer and call may be implicit, but on the Augustinian principles that underlie Rahner's thought here, any experience of a call to self-transcendence and positive response to it comes as a result of and is an encounter with God's grace. The ultimate grace, however, the fulfillment of grace in this world, is being possessed by the very presence of God in eternity.

What then is grace? Surely it is all of these, and no one of these positive affirmations of what grace is should be taken as excluding any other. Each of these understandings has an internal logic of its own, as was seen. Only with the most extreme care and reticence should these positive understandings, and the experiences that they reflect, be seen as exclusive and used negatively to affirm what grace is not. This is not to deny that every specific positive understanding is by that very fact affirmative and therefore limiting and exclusive of counter positions. One *can* say what God, what human existence, and what our relationship with God, are not. But this can be done of another Christian affirmation only if one understands exactly what it means and in terms of that particular language.

The Effects of Grace

There are two truths about history, both of them absolute, and they apply as well to the history of the Christian theology of grace. The first truth is that history never repeats itself. The second truth is that history always repeats itself. On the one hand, seeing the twists and turns that history takes relativizes particular languages of grace and invites us to understand in our own terms. On the other hand, all these past languages deal precisely with grace in Christian terms, that is, God's love as manifested in Christ in a point of time and experienced through the same Spirit that was in Christ Jesus. It is to be expected, then, that beneath the varied languages and accents there be common themes, normative themes, that should find their place in every account of grace and any present-day understanding of grace. One should try, then, to point to what seem to be some of the essential effects of grace in Christian life as they have been consistently manifested in Christian experience and articulated in Christian theology and doctrine.

Forgiving

God's love for people as manifested in Christ and as experienced in his grace is merciful and forgiving. This theme is highlighted in Luther's theology and in Lutheran tradition, but it is commonly present in all the theologies of grace. In Trent, grace is justifying, a passing out of a state of sin into a state of being forgiven. Justification is the first effect of grace in Aquinas. In Augustine the theme of forgiving does not dominate, but it is clearly present especially in his consideration of baptism. The theme is also present in Rahner who in his later writings constantly refers to grace as both elevating and forgiving.

Given human existence as it is in the world, one of the primary obstacles to salvation is its sheer unworthiness. No truly religious experience of God can lack some sense of the dichotomy between what human existence is and what it ought to be, and of its utter lack of holiness (wholeness) before the living God. And depending on one's religious sensibility and profundity, one can come to realize the extent to which the human person is hopelessly and inextricably immersed in a situation of sin that is not only exterior but also internal to us. It is for this reason that Christ, his grace and his salvation appear essentially connected with forgiveness. He came to call sinners and we are "prodigal sons." "Forgive us our trespasses" is part of the Christian's prayer. An essential theme of the good news of the Gospel is the grace of mercy that forgives. And here grace will be experienced more intensely the more our basic unworthiness itself is experienced.

Healing

God's love for a person is manifested as a positive force in his or her life that heals and cures the sickness that is selfishness and enables one to love God in return. This theme dominates Augustine's theology of grace and is his permanent legacy to the formal doctrine of grace. Human freedom is bound; one cannot freely act for unselfish motives; we cannot love God unless we experience the healing love of the God who first loves us. Again, any realization of this aspect of grace and the necessity of it can only come as a function of the profoundest questioning about human life and motivation. Why is there goodness at all, Augustine asked. And the Christian response is that altruism and true self-transcendence can only come through God's impelling it and drawing it out of a person, by drawing human existence out of itself.

The theme runs large in the New Testament, especially in Paul and in John. Why is it that a person does what he or she does not want to do, and does not do what he or she knows should be done? In Paul, knowledge is not virtue. The virtuous life is only possible through the Spirit of love poured out in a person's heart. If Christians are those who love one another, this can only be through the experience of the power of grace.

Elevating

In every language of grace, the effect of God's love for human existence is described in one way or another as elevating. This is expressed in the sharpest and clearest terms in Aquinas, where grace elevates human life not only to a new level in the hierarchy of beings, but even to a sharing in the divine nature itself. Participation in the love of God manifested in Christ means participating in, sharing, being flooded with, God's own life. And whether the language here be ontological or mystical, it is not devoid of experience. All religious experiences of grace share in some degree the note of being elevated by contact and union with God through his love.[5]

This theme, then, in whatever language it is spoken, merely reasserts what is announced in the New Testament. Such images as "rebirth," the "new being," in whom "Christ lives," "sons of God" meant for resurrection, all indicate a qualitative change in human existence and a level of life that is qualitatively different from and higher than life untouched by the gift of God's grace. And the mystical language of John and Paul, of "remaining in" Christ and being "incorporated" into his body, is especially relevant to this theme of participating in divine life.

Freeing

Perhaps the most important effect of the experience of God's love is freedom. This freedom is indeed a function of the other three effects of grace and includes them. God's grace frees people from their sin; it frees them from themselves by liberating the will to act; it frees them from the world and all fear of it because it bestows on them a value that transcends the finitude of this world. And over and above this, contact with God's love in grace engenders a security and self-possession that frees a person for others and for the world.

It is not surprising that the image of freedom dominates the biblical understanding of salvation and grace. From the freedom from bondage and captivity in the Exodus to the freedom from sin and even death in Christ, the idea of what God communicates to human existence by his love is crystallized in the theme of freedom. In a sense a longing for freedom is the most fundamental of all human aspirations. It means movement, fulness of life and vital activity, self-creation and fulfillment, spiritual expansiveness, full possession even in diffusion. It takes the love of God for human beings to complete such a human longing. It is not something that we can attain for ourselves. Indeed, the doctrine of grace is the teaching that God bestowed this infinite longing so that he could fulfill it with his grace.

The Christian Life

It is a small step from the topic of the effects of grace in Christian life to a consideration of the Christian life itself. As was said in chapter 1, one of the basic issues of the theology of grace is spirituality, a fundamental understanding of the meaning and dynamics of the Christian life. It is appropriate therefore that a summary of the theology of grace as it operates in personal life be given in terms of Christian experience of the Christian life.

The symbol "liberation" is fitting to interpret the effects of grace in Christian life and experience and it is chosen as a unifying category. If as was just said it is true that freedom is the most all-embracing effect of grace, then the symbol liberation cannot be too far off the mark. The word liberation is a substantive form of the verb meaning to set free, to release from restraint or bondage. As a verbal symbol it embodies a host of meanings that cluster around various experiences of freedom, autonomy and human liberty. Surely the experience of God's grace will entail some form or forms of liberation.

The term liberation is chosen as a central symbol for interpreting the experience of grace for several further reasons. God's grace and salvation have always been conceived of in terms approaching some form of liberation as the words "salvation" and "redemption" themselves indicate. And shifting to the present, the experiences of freedom and liberation in various forms are very much part of modern culture. The consciousness of being in history and the relative freedom from the past that historical consciousness mediates, the experience of human autonomy and a new ability and responsibility to control, in some measure, both nature and history, the tendency to define the very nature of the human person as freedom, all these cultural factors make the symbol liberation very germane to modern culture and at the same time pose the question of the relation between these experiences and the effects of grace.

The symbol liberation is used heuristically, that is, we shall try to inform the term liberation with the content and meaning that is given by the history of the theology of grace. This does not make Augustine, for example, a liberation theologian in the contemporary sense of that title. Quite the contrary; the goal is to discover what Augustine said in terms of liberation and consequently the meaning of liberating grace in the theologies of the past. The method then is one of retrieval that both interprets the past history of the theology of grace from a contemporary point of view and fully allows contemporary affirmations to be informed by the Christian experience of the past.

The question, then, is this: How are we to describe Christian experience and the Christian life, in short, Christian spirituality, in terms of the liberating power of grace?

Liberation from Oneself

Although present as well in the other authors, this experience of grace stands out in Luther because of the personalistic manner in which he frames his understanding. Through faith one receives forgiveness and acceptance by a divine and cosmic power with the tenderness of a personal God. In the experience of God's grace, God's favor, benevolence, mercy and love, a person is accepted precisely as he or she is, in spite of unworthiness and sin. In psychological terms, just as a person gains his or her identity in others' reaction or response, so here the Christian gains an "absolute identity," one that is ultimately positive, even though it includes judgment, because of God's love. Persons can accept themselves, both their present and their past, in spite of the finitude, sin, irresponsibility, that have gone to constitute the self. This is an enormously liberating experience. And in places Luther's description of this experience of grace, although he uses a vastly different language, is remarkably close to the effects of grace as seen by Aquinas in such terms as "elevation," "divinization" and "participation" in the divine life. By an almost mystical union with Christ, according to Luther, and in a love relationship symbolized in a bridal image, the liberation from self transforms Christian life into life on another plane.[6]

Liberation from Sin

Augustine too described the experience of grace as a liberation from sin but in a way quite different from that of Luther. Here sin is seen as egoism. By sin is meant the turning of human motive and intention and consequent behavior back in upon itself so that value outside the self is not enjoyed in itself but used for the self. The person as a center of consciousness is a center of reality and what is beyond the self is drawn into the self and exists for the self. Sin is thus both a mode of existence and the activities flowing from this stance of autonomy and hubris. Human freedom is trapped or bound *within itself* so that self-transcendence, any desire for the good as such, is impossible. Grace breaks this self-enclosed state of human existence. Grace liberates human freedom from sin by engendering in the personality, in the human mind and will, a delight and desire transcending the self and responding to value outside the self and for its own sake. Augustine is most explicit about this liberating experience of grace in the actual moment of conversion and in the life of the believer who lives his life for God. But at the same time he recognized experiences before his own final Christian conversion as impulses of grace causing self-transcendence.[7] Thus the working of grace and its liberating effect is a process that need not be limited in such a way that God is seen as the only explicit motive for acting, need not be limited to the realm of explicitly religious experience, although this indeed is its goal.

Freedom to Love

In Augustine the freedom to love is simply the other side of freedom from sin. Grace does not destroy free choice; on the contrary, it establishes it, expands its horizon and guarantees it. Quite consistently with contemporary understanding, Augustine saw the human personality as a mixture of freedom and determinism. Such was the power of habit and custom to bind freedom itself from within that despite the power to choose this or that object, it is not in the power of freedom to love authentically. God alone through the power of his grace enables freedom to love. This freedom to love—liberty, as Augustine called it—does not strictly speaking add to or multiply the concrete opportunities or objects of free decision. Rather grace releases freedom from its inner constrictions and positively gives it a new horizon and scope, a new motive. The power to love, to delight in good and value outside the self and ultimately the supreme good, God, engenders a whole new existence in a person precisely by altering his fundamental orientation. Grace literally frees one from all objective law because the very ideal that the law points to becomes internalized; the Spirit of love is the generating force of behavior. Quite simply, grace is the force of God working in human existence moving it in love.

Liberation from Nature

In Aquinas, the reason why human beings need grace is that they do not have the power within themselves to achieve the goal for which they were intended, that is, the utterly transcendent goal of union with God. Human nature is a capacity for personal communion with God even while the active power to achieve this is lacking. This new principle of activity is grace. Grace thus liberates the human person from finitude, from the limited and limiting aspects of his nature. The expansive power, both as a habit and as a *motus*,[8] opens up human being-in-this-world to a higher possibility, to a higher form of activity and love that is destined for a goal that utterly transcends native possibilities, namely, personal union with God.

Liberation from Fear of the World

This important theme of liberation from the world is found in all theologies of grace but is most clearly expressed in Luther. By one's union with Christ through grace one shares in Christ's kingship, so that "every Christian is by faith so exalted above all things that, by virtue of a spiritual power, he is lord of all things."[9] This is not a physical power, but power springing from union with God as transcendent and absolute. As mentioned earlier, in very different terms but expressive of the same theme, Aquinas speaks of being raised up or elevated by grace in such a way that one participates in divine life; one shares a divine kind of existence. The taking cognizance of this union with God in religious experience is at the same time a relativizing experience of everything that is finite. Grace therefore frees one from all fear of the world; it is a relativization of every cultural product and a liberation from ultimate fear of every human institution. The world and its history as Rahner puts it are demythologized and demystified.

Liberation from Death

The human person, according to Augustine, desires to be. The internal desire not to cease to exist with time as all other things do, not to pass away but to be permanently, incorruptibly, absolutely and eternally, grounds the dynamism of life itself. Grace, responding to that desire, both by turning one toward God and acting as the medium of the experience of God, liberates from death and establishes human being as autonomous. "If you begin by wishing to exist, and add a desire for fuller and fuller existence, you rise in the scale, and are furnished for life that supremely is."[10] Of course death, and the suffering in this world that is an integral part of death, must still be undergone. And death retains its threatening and fearful aspect, but not ultimately so. To the extent that one is grasped by God's grace and surrenders to it, in the same measure can death be met with peace. Grace liberates from the ultimate terror of death and transforms it from a passion into an action. It liberates also from the terror of time and history, and releases constructive energy in a context of hope.

Liberation of God (and His Designs)

Liberation *from* is also a liberation *for*. In all theologies of grace the experience of grace is a liberation for God. In Augustine, through grace one loves God as the source and ground of all goodness. In Aquinas one's whole nature is recreated through its permanent attitudes (virtues) and in its action toward union with God. In Luther one is by grace already united with God and thus saved; but from a good tree good fruits come. One may add that liberation for

God is a liberation that enables God's will to be done. Grace liberates human beings for the designs of God.

Liberation for the Neighbor

Although explained in different ways by different theologies of grace, liberation for the neighbor appears in all as an essential element and in some the very criterion for the operation of grace in human life. In Aquinas grace informs the whole person and in the will it appears as charity. And charity, which is primarily love of God, plays itself out toward salvation through the moral life of love of neighbor. This conception has the advantage of integrating grace into the whole of life as it moves through history. In Luther, however, the liberating effect of grace for the neighbor is dramatically and idealistically represented. An essential component of God's grace is a spontaneously and utterly gratuitous, altruistic love of neighbor. *Caritas* in Luther means primarily love of neighbor, and one does not love the neighbor in order to love God, nor does one love God through the neighbor. Rather, having received grace a person is internally liberated and turns to the neighbor for his own sake. The Christian is a servant without desire for reward. In Rahner, finally, love of God and love of neighbor, although they can be distinguished objectively, tend to merge into a single transcendental reality of self-transcending experience at the very deepest level of experience. And here one has rejoined the Augustinian existential tradition: Where there is self-transcendence, there is the movement of grace.

Liberation for the World and History

The affirmation that grace effects a liberation in human personality for the world and for history is both a climax of the summary of the personal experience of grace and an introduction to our final chapter. The discussion has centered up to now on the effects of grace within the human person and in personal life; indeed, the theology of grace is narrowly focused on the personal reality of grace. But at the same time the effects of grace include a liberating or opening out of personal existence to God and his designs, to the neighbor, and consequently to the world understood as other people in history. Salvation as it is begun in this world in a life under the influence of grace is a concrete, visible and external life lived among other people in a public way. To say that the effects of grace are lives lived for the world and for history, therefore, is to shift the whole context of the discussion to that of the public or historical effects of grace, the question of the history of salvation, the social manifestations of grace and a theology of history. It is to this that we now turn.

Notes

1. See chapter 1, pp. 24–29.

2. "God is real since he produces real effects"(William James, *The Varieties of Religious Experience* [New York: Collier Books, 1961], p. 400. See pp. 399–400).

3. It should always be noted that this is a strictly dialectical assertion. In Rahner's view, which is consonant with James on this point, while grace is experienced, it is not experienced *as grace*. The effects of grace are experienced precisely as anthropological or psychological experiences, within human consciousness, and thus it is equally true that grace as an object is not directly experienced. The experience of grace is always a *human experience*, and it is always subject to illusion.

4. This Augustinian problematic is a tacit presupposition of Rahner's doctrine of the supernatural existential and of his explanation of *how* grace is made universally effective in human experience, that is, anonymously through the will. Ultimately, his doctrine may be characterized as "justification through love."

5. Cf. William James, "Mysticism" in *The Varieties of Religious Experience*, pp. 229–336.

6. See chapter 4, pp. 96–97.

7. For example, what may in effect be called Augustine's first conversion to "truth" was a self-transcending experience he credited to God's grace. See *The Confessions of St. Augustine*, bk. III, chap. 4 (Garden City, N.Y.: Image Books, Doubleday, 1960), pp. 81–82.

8. See chapter 3, pp. 66–67.

9. See chapter 4, pp. 97–98.

10. Augustine, *On Free Will*, bk. III, vii, 21, in *Augustine: Earlier Writings*, ed. John H. S. Burleigh (Philadelphia: Westminster Press, 1953), p. 405.

8
Social Grace:
A Liberationist Theology of History

The modern conception of human existence is characterized by a historical consciousness, a consciousness of being in history. Moreover, it is taken for granted that human beings in some degree have responsibility for history, otherwise the many expressions either implicit or explicit of guilt for certain human conditions would make no sense. In some degree human beings can control history, modify its course, alter its conditions. Human history is an opening toward the future and all share the responsibility to make it a better world and a better future for others with us and after us. So strongly is this responsibility felt by many, and so enormous the project it entails, that it is often accompanied by an unwillingness to be distracted from the task, especially by religion.[1] Thus the other side of historical consciousness and its sense of autonomy is the secularized consciousness. By this is meant a feeling of being at home in this world and in time, a loss of an interventionist God who will solve our problems, a view of the world as the raw material for human creativity.

These developments have in turn placed a considerable burden on the self-understanding of Christianity, which has in the past been overly concerned with private life and a personal salvation that practically speaking referred to life after death. Many of our conceptions from the past, which we are quite rightly slow in changing but must change nevertheless, so stress a mythic conception of God and our absolute dependence on his interventions that they are in almost visible conflict with that other everyday conception of reality. Culture thus has forced Christian theology to look again at the doctrines of eschatology, the doctrines of salvation and salvation history, the doctrine of how grace is operative in the world and in human history at large, the doctrine of the Christian life. We are less inclined to accept cosmological theories of salvation or redemption at face value or uncritically, or to imagine God entering history in a visible and direct way as an additional factor in a chain of events.[2] If God works in history it must be in and through the agency of the human beings who make history. And God's objective salvation must be seen first of all and concretely as the effects of God's grace, first in human community in a personalist sense and then in wider "objective" societal structures that obtain through history. To grasp objective salvation, that is, salvation going on outside the individual as an a priori invitation, one must begin by seeing grace working publicly in history.

The question that will be addressed in this last chapter thus concerns the public working of grace. Can saving grace be understood in a way that furthers social responsibility? And can this grace be seen further as a factor underlying the external and public events of history? And, finally, is such a view totally discontinuous with previous theologies of grace or can Christian tradition be adapted without violence to this new historical context that increasingly forms the matrix for our understanding?

Method

In this effort to construct a contemporary language of grace in keeping with a concern for understanding history, once again we have chosen the symbol "liberation" as a key concept. One reason for this is certainly the prevalence of a number of liberation theologies that are current. But right at the outset we wish to enter a distinction between the theology of liberation, or the many theologies of liberation of particular authors, and the liberationist interpretation of Christianity. Every particular understanding of Christianity is and should be deeply incarnated or inculturated in the particular situation of the people out of which it emerges and which it seeks to address. This is particularly true of the liberation theologies that have integrated into their method of understanding Christianity social, economic, political and cultural analyses of the world in which they arise. But precisely to the degree to which a theology of liberation is bound to a situation that is peculiar or unique, that theology is not exportable to an area where the social and cultural conditions are different.[3] For this reason we speak of the liberationist interpretation of Christianity in an effort to look for that properly Christian component that lies beneath any particular liberation theology. The liberationist interpretation of Christianity attempts to deal with that which is distinctively Christian and therefore universal to Christian faith itself in whatever part of the world and in conjunction with whatever particular social analysis that may be used.[4]

While this distinction is helpful, there is still more to be said, and other questions to be answered. The liberationist interpretation of Christianity presents Christian salvation in such a way that it is seen as intrinsically and fundamentally, although not exclusively, related to and having bearing upon life in this world in all of its forms and activities. Even granting the distinction just mentioned, it is still not commonly agreed by general Christian consciousness that Christian salvation includes this intraworldly and historical dimension as an essential and constitutive one.[5] The question that is raised, therefore, is whether or not this claim of liberation theology is true, and in what sense. Is the liberationist interpretation really a theology at all, or is it simply a movement that is more or less a product of culture but supporting itself extrinsically with Christian idealism and rhetoric? Is the liberationist interpretation of Christianity really a social movement that has adapted Christian language and slogans in order to seek its particular goals? Or, on the contrary, is this really a theology and therefore a statement of a universally normative dimension of Christian faith and life? Can one say, finally, that today the Christian symbol "salvation" is intrinsically and essentially bound up with liberation?

In order to make this claim convincingly one must address history, the history of Christian faith experience. That is to say, if this understanding is correct, it cannot be a totally new claim, one that is alien to or lacks all continuity with the tradition of Christian self-understanding. More positively, one must be able to show how, whether implicitly or explicitly, Christian self-understanding has included a basic dimension aptly termed liberation in its conception of salvation. The question of this chapter, therefore, is this: What exactly is the connection between Christian salvation and liberation?

The fundamental theological interpretation on which many theologies of liberation depend is either a close association between or an identification of the two Christian symbols, salvation and liberation.[6] If Christian salvation and liberation are intimately related, then it is certainly true that one cannot consider Christianity apart from a deep interest in human liberation. Obviously this connection depends on the exact meaning that one assigns the two symbols. But in practically every case the exact relation between salvation, which in Christianity is a "purely religious" concept insofar as God alone saves, and human liberation especially on the social, economic and political levels remains fuzzy or unclear. And this has abetted the suspicions that it is other than strictly religious motives and theological reasons that underlie this theology.

We believe, however, that the theology of grace, even as we have developed it in its long history thus far, contains the link between the concepts of salvation and liberation.[7] And it is on this premise that this final discussion of public or social grace and a liberationist theology of history is constructed.

Salvation Is Grace

The primary symbol or type for salvation in the religion of the Old Testament is "exodus." There one has a people freed from bondage or captivity or slavery to a foreign master and entering into a new relationship with God, a new life of chosenness and predilection by God symbolized in a covenant. What really happened back then, if one might pose that irreverent question; or, since that question cannot be answered historically, what may we suppose to have happened? Undoubtedly there was a historical event, an escape, and a newly won freedom on the part of this people. And coupled with this Scripture testifies to the vivid realization that whatever happened to this people transcended their own capacity for freedom and power of self-determination; it was a gift, something received from God; it was grace.[8] Here one has the basis to determine the essential characteristics of the notion of salvation. Certainly the word itself includes the idea of "being freed from" and "being freed for." Moreover, it was and is essentially religious. This means that salvation refers first of all to historical events and experiences that transcend human capacity and that are celebrated as God acting in history.[9]

These qualities are epitomized in the New Testament faith in Jesus as the Christ. For the Christian, in the advent of Jesus, his life, death and resurrection, one has the concrete and unsurpassable event in history manifesting the saving love of God for the human race. He is the Christ; he is savior. In the terms of Karl Rahner, Christ is the definitive real symbol of God's saving grace. And in the power of God's freely bestowed love or grace mediated through him we are freed from sin, from the Law, from the power of evil itself, and from death. In him God's universal salvific will is revealed. God's actual saving activity for all peoples of all time is made known; in short, the force and power of God's active love for all mankind and history itself is shown to us. In the words of Paul: God "has made known to us in all wisdom and insight the mystery of his will, according to his purpose which he set forth in Christ as a place for the fulness of time, to unite all things to him, things in heaven and things on earth" (Eph. 1:9–10).

Grace, as we have seen throughout this book, is nothing other than God's active love for humankind. When one addresses salvation in terms of the symbol "grace," there are two consequences that should be noted. First of all, the primary emphasis falls on what has classically been called subjective as opposed to objective redemption. In this way, then, theories of objective redemption, many of which tend toward anthropomorphism and mythology, will be left aside.[10] When salvation is conceived of in terms of grace, one focuses on the concrete and historical manifestations of the effects of God's saving love within the Christian economy. This is certainly the dominant concept of the New Testament itself, for the primitive community of faith was constituted by the pouring out of the Spirit and lived in the experiential enthusiasm of its gifts and charisms. Here then salvation appears as an economy, a working of God in a history of human events.

The other side of this approach is that salvation is viewed in terms of its breaking forth in this world. Certainly the meaning of salvation is eschatological. Ultimately, salvation cannot but reach its climax in the end-time and on the other side of history, both for the individual and for the race, without at the same time being undermined in its very foundation. However, it must also be said that *that* salvation is begun now and is taking place within history. Salvation, although it is the end of history, can only be conceived of by human beings within history and as being worked out now through history. Tradition has generally maintained that there is a continuity between the human person in his entirety now and he who is saved; and there is a continuity between the love of God experienced now (grace) and final union with God. Without such a continuity life in this world cannot be conceived of as having an ultimate intrinsic value or worth. Therefore, while from one limited point of view life in this world and history may seem minimized relative to eschatological salvation, in fact it is maximized. For on the one hand, without God's grace (salvation), what ceases to exist in this world passes permanently out of existence. And on the other, what is caught up in God's love (grace) in this world will remain. The history of salvation in this world is strictly speaking continuous with eschatological salvation, to the same extent that it will be transformed.

Actual salvation, then, as it occurs in history may be identified with what has classically been called grace in the history of theology. We have already seen in the last chapter that grace is liberating on the personal level of human existence. It now remains to begin to interpret once again the history of the theology of grace to show how these liberating effects have an impact on the public, "objective" and social level of history.

Rahner on Grace in the World and in History

As was seen in chapter 6, much of Rahner's early theology is an effort to mediate between the Scholastic theology that preceded him and the modern world. There are three themes, generally accepted today, from his theology of grace that may serve as an introduction to the further consideration of grace in the context of history.

The first point is Rahner's conception of the unity of the natural and graced orders of human existence. He argues this position from the doctrine of the universal salvific will of God. Given this teaching from Christ's revelation, one must also affirm that human nature or the human person is different from what he would have been had not God willed salvation since human existence is totally dependent on God's will and intention. Human "nature," then, as it actually exists, must be under the influence of its "supernatural" end, goal and calling. Human existence embodies within itself a tendency or dynamism or positive drive for its salvific end, a dynamism that is itself grace or a gift, but that informs all human-being. In this way Rahner breaks down every dualistic conception of the natural sphere and that of grace, the kingdom of humankind and the kingdom of God, the secular or profane and the religious. Grace is part of the whole of human life and existence in all its aspects. One must view the whole of the human sphere, the world, positively because it is under the influence of grace.[11] Grace is one with human nature and inextricably interwoven with human life and activity. In no way, except where it is a sinful rejection of grace, can the world or life in it be viewed negatively. Its very existence is grounded in an offer of a personal encounter with God, which is grace.[12]

A second contribution of Rahner is his explanation of the unity of profane and salvation history, which in a sense is a mere corollary of the former thesis that emerges when it is placed in the context of history. Given God's universal salvific will, it must follow that every single being has an actual and concrete opportunity or occasion to encounter saving grace; otherwise, the universal salvific will of God would make no sense. Rahner explains how this can occur through a conception of implicit revelation and implicit faith; whenever a person transcends himself in a moral act he is implicitly responding to God's self-communication or offer of himself in grace. In this way any radical dualism between secular and general salvation history is broken down. There is but one history. The history of the race we know, and the whole of this history, is a history of salvation grounded and supported throughout its length by the permanent, ever-active and effective offer of God's grace. And as a Christian one must believe that this grace ultimately triumphs over the petty evil of human beings. In short, one cannot a priori and consistently view secular history and its human mechanisms negatively.[13]

One last theme from Rahner's theology of grace will lead to a consideration of some formal theses for a theology of history. Rahner is insistent on the fact that one's encounter with salvation occurs in one's encounter with the everyday world. Without prejudice to organized religious or church life, "it occurs always in an encounter with the world and not merely in the confined sector of the sacred or of worship and 'religion' in the narrow sense; it occurs in encounters with one's neighbor, with one's historical task, with the so-called world of everyday life, in and with what we call the history of the individual and of communities."[14] This is so because salvation and grace are really identical. "Grace is really this salvation itself, for it is God himself in his forgiving and divinizing love."[15] This concrete existential and historical point of view also allows Rahner to understand God's universal and eternal saving will and the concrete offer of his divinizing and forgiving self-communication, that is, his actual self-communication in history, as materially unified, coextensive and mutually causative. God's universal saving will causes saving history, and actual salvation history is the ground of this saving will, so that actual historical salvation *is* in this sense the saving will of God itself.[16] From this perspective it follows that a theology of history or saving history cannot really be established by a priori reasoning. In formulating a material theology of history, one must look at the actual events of history, both inside the religions and beyond them, as well as at Christianity. But at the same time, relying on a theology of grace and viewing the effects of grace in an experiential and quasi-empirical way, one can outline some formal theses or themes relative to how and where this saving history becomes manifest.

Themes for a Liberationist Theology of History

Within the context of the evaluation of the world and of history as found implied in Rahner's theology of grace, what can be said from the history of the theology of grace that has bearing on an interpretation of God's grace working in history? In what way can grace, or God acting through his grace, be seen as operative in society and history, and this in a liberating way? By answering these questions we approach a liberationist interpretation of salvation history.

Grace as a Liberation from the World and for the Neighbor

As a first theme, clearly present in Luther's theology of grace, grace as a liberation from the world and for the neighbor is most important and fundamental. The contact with God mediated through Christian revelation or through any religious experience that in Christian understanding may be called an effect of God's grace relativizes the world and history precisely insofar as one is grasped by the transcendence of God. At the same time, one is liberated in gratitude for dedicated service to the neighbor in Luther's terms; one is freed for self-transcending love in Augustine's. Although formulated as a personal experience here, in fact there will be no such thing as a liberation movement for others unless there are internally liberated people who are freed from this world and fear of its powers and institutions. There can be no authentic or altruistic action for others that is not ultimately the result of God's internal liberating grace. Thus what seems at first sight to be a personal effect of grace really in its full dimensions essentially interpersonal. The effect of grace is essentially social, and urges human personality toward expansiveness and self-transcendence.

God Acts in Loving Human Freedom

This assertion is based on Augustine's and afterwards the Christian doctrine of the necessity of prevenient grace for any and all self-transcending and saving acts of love. To appreciate this insight one must ask, as Augustine did, the simple but fundamental question of why there is or how there could be any authentic moral goodness or love at all in this world. Relying on his own personal experience as well as on Scripture (for Scripture reveals both sin and grace correlatively), Augustine responded with his doctrine of the absolute priority of grace. From this it follows that God and his grace are at the root of all love in this world; wherever there is authentic love in this world, there God is acting. This is the precise point of his argument against Pelagius. And here one has a first principle for understanding how God acts in history without resorting to either anthropomorphic or interventionist views of God performing on the same level as other causes in the chain of natural events. God's grace, God's effective presence, is the driving and sustaining force of all human goodness and love, and this is the ultimate basis of every form of authentic human community, no matter how basic and natural any particular communitarian form may seem.[17]

God Acting in the World

That it is God who is at work in the world in loving human freedom is strengthened by Aquinas's notion of cooperative grace.

Under the category "operative grace" Aquinas examines the effects of grace within the human personality, namely, justification and sanctification. "Cooperative grace" refers to the effects of grace as it is seen flowing through human freedom out into the world and the public sphere in action.[18] There can be no danger of Pelagianism here when one grasps the fact that this whole dynamism from start to finish is initiated and sustained by the impulse and drawing of God's grace.[19] In this way, in the lives of the prophets, the saints and every self-transcending person, grace or God's action breaks through into the public sphere of everyday life and becomes visible, tangible, concrete and real in the world. After William James, one must say that the saints are the authors and increasers of goodness in the world; they make ideals visible for society and they actualize them in history.[20] The life of a self-transcending person dedicated to the concerns of the unfortunate ones in society is an "effective ferment of goodness" and a "slow transmuter of the earthly into a more heavenly order."[21] Such lives are the agents of God's action in the world; one might even say that they constitute the way God acts in history.

God's Action for God's Designs

Another theme from Aquinas may be exploited for a theology of history. Obviously one does not find a strong sense of history in Saint Thomas in the contemporary sense of our historical consciousness and sensibility of process moving toward an open future. On the contrary, his whole theology of grace is firmly structured by teleology, and teleology is quite different from eschatology. But since they are structurally cousins, it would not be illegitimate to transform Aquinas's teleological affirmations into the context of collective human history. In Aquinas one has the basic affirmation, in TeSelle's words, "that grace opens up a possibility which does not lie within the scope of man's natural powers and is not implied by his being as a man."[22] In a historical and eschatological context a doctrine of cooperative grace implies that, through grace and people animated by grace, possibilities in and through history tending toward God's design in history, but not possible by human powers alone, are opened up and worked out by God through graced human agency. In scriptural language, God's action in and through human loving is moving toward the goal of his kingdom, the kingdom of communion, harmony, peace and reconciliation. Certainly this is not observable in history on the grand scale nor does it imply a notion of steady progress. It is an object of faith. And when it occurs, even in a partial way, it is precisely the work of grace since such a goal manifestly exceeds human capabilities.

It may be well here to consider for a moment Luther's theology of grace because he departs from Aquinas (and Augustine) precisely on this point of teleological dynamism.[23] There seem to be even less grounds in Luther for a theology of history than in Aquinas because for him one is saved now, already, in an actual interpersonal relationship with God through Christ's word. Moreover, there is a tendency to distinguish the graced person from his works, his faith in God from his life in the world, the two kingdoms. In Luther, freedom and action for the neighbor are not in themselves salvific but rather presuppose salvation and flow from it. These strong distinctions by Luther were felt to be necessary during his time in order to absolutely rule out every kind of Pelagianism in the theology of grace. After that is admitted, and assuming an existential and historical point of view, one must affirm that there can be no radical distinction between what a person is and what he does; the two are mutually implied in each other. But in the existential order one can combine the Thomistic and Lutheran emphases in an already–not yet tension that responds in a salutary manner to the question of understanding the Christian life in the broader context of history.[24] "Already": We are saved already by God's forgiveness and this gives the Christian an absolute freedom sustained by grace to respond to the neighbor. If there is no salvation experienced in faith now, there can be no ground for hope in the future. Thus salvation experienced now through grace is a precondition for freedom to turn to the world and its future. "Not yet": At the same time we are not yet either personally or as a group or as a race saved. What we are now must be sustained by grace in our action and this action is likewise constitutive of our being. Thus Lutheran and Thomistic spiritualities can be seen as complementary and, held in tension, they serve to correct the dangers on both sides.

A Liberationist Theology of History

Personal sin is overcome by grace both because it is God's per-

sonal forgiveness and the transforming power of his Spirit turning
egocentrism into love. But in order to build a theological understanding of history, one must pass from the level of the interpersonal to
the more general and objective level of the collective, societal and
public. Here one encounters the concept of "social sin." The notion
of social sin is highly paradoxical and complex and the few remarks
made here will scarcely do justice to the reality. This brief analysis is
meant simply as a general definition to engender clarity in the discussion since the concept of social sin is frequently abused.

Social Sin

The prime analogue for "sin" is personal sin, and this may be
understood objectively as a human action that hurts or injures another person or the self. Sin is also "against God" as it were indirectly, that is, because both the actor and the person offended are God's
own, the injury is against his loving will. Second, and much more
basically, sin refers to selfish acts and the basic egoism from which
they flow. Here sin is defined subjectively and appears both as an
inner condition of human existence and as the source out of which
objective sin flows. Autonomous freedom inherently tends toward
making the self a kind of center of all reality. Consequently one fails
at self-transcendence, fails to recogize and respond to value outside
the self; sin uses other persons as means for self-enhancement. Sinful
behavior can be seen as an attempt to draw the outer world into the
self in a more or less conscious effort at subjugation. Third, that
which makes sin strictly speaking sin and not simply an evil is consciousness and responsibility. The Scholastic distinction between material and formal sin is useful here. That which the concept of morality adds to law is precisely freedom and responsibility. One should
only speak of sin properly so-called when there is some element of
knowledge, freedom, intention and responsibility, for guilt, which is
the correlate of sin, can only be a function of responsible freedom.[25]

What can be said of personal sin can also be said of social sin,
but *only* analogously. The ability to make this transition to a concept
of social sin at all rests on two primal suppositions. The first is the
phenomenon of interdependence and the fact that human existence is
essentially social. There is no such thing as total human indepen-
dence; on every level of existence, although on some levels more than
others, there is an interlocking of human subjects with the result that

our actions always influence others. The second supposition is that the systems of culture and society that govern or pattern this interaction are created and sustained by human beings themselves. From the most general and deepest level of culture, as a system of meanings and values, to the most particular of institutions that regulate human interchange, social structures have their origin in and continue to exist through the agency of human wills. As Peter Berger puts it: "Despite the objectivity that marks the social world we experience, it does not thereby acquire an ontological status apart from the human creativity that produced it [and continues to sustain it]."[26]

To proceed with the analogy, then, because the social systems or institutions by which human affairs are structured are not part of nature but functions of human freedom and able to be changed, insofar as they victimize, oppress or are generally harmful and damaging to persons, they are sinful at least in an objective or material sense. Second, the intentional creation of and knowingly deliberate participation in institutions that are harmful to and destructive of human life is sinful in an exact sense of the term, that is, subjectively and formally. But here it is most important to note that these institutions depend on wills *collectively*, and that groups, institutions and societies do not have an internal consciousness and center of freedom in the same way that a human person does. Therefore the *kind* of personal responsibility is radically different from that involved in one's control over the self and the *degree* of personal responsibility will vary enormously according to the level of participation and the ability to alter a situation. For example, some social institutions, such as language, become so instinctively internalized that they function almost like "second nature."

When one considers all these factors at once it becomes evident that social sin is somewhat paradoxical. For to the extent that behavior becomes purely social, that is, routinized, unreflective and objective, it ceases in the same measure to be formally sinful and approaches an objectively evil situation. Precisely insofar as sin is social it must be revealed or disclosed as sin to human consciousnesses.[27] Moreover, there are probably very few or no social insititutions that do not discriminate and cause harm to some people. All human beings, then, are caught in a web of social sin and all suffer implicitly or explicitly from guilt and need deliverance, salvation and liberation. But over and above this general condition, there are many instances of blatantly selfish institutions that with a more or less explicit intent oppress and destroy some to the benefit of others. Even here one has to be careful in assigning guilt or judging intentions. On the one hand, because of interdependence one can kill from afar with no knowledge or awareness or intention. On the other hand, by definition all responsibility for social sin is shared responsibility within a wide spectrum of degree. Because institutions and systems always appear objective relative to individual awareness or power of action, general prophetic denunciations and accusations often meet resistance where a reasoned appeal to good will might not.

God's Action through Grace against Sin

In the light of the themes gathered from the history of the theology of grace and given the concept of social sin presented here, we can now go on to propose some theses regarding how God acts in history against sin in a liberating way.

First of all, the saving and liberating effect of grace occurs primarily in the individual personality.[28] In the inner life of the person, salvation and liberation from sin are materially and formally identical. This first proposition prevents the confusion of an immediate identification of liberating grace with an external personal or social liberation. One must affirm that a person who lives in prison or slavery can still be saved in a religious sense both in this world and ultimately. Inversely, a person externally free and affluent may be deprived of inner salvific freedom. Thus the transition from poverty or oppression to wealth and political freedom should not be confused *tout court* with the salvation of that subject in the Christian view. But this is not an affirmation denying any connection between grace and political or social freedom, as will be shown in what follows.

Second, action for liberation of others on the part of any person, or participation in liberation movements, witnesses first of all to his or her own salvation or salvific liberation. Such social action, if it is authentic, is salvific liberation first of all for the participants themselves. Here liberation refers to the self-transcendence that is intrinsic to the saving faith that is informed by and works through charity in Roman Catholic terms, or in the freedom for self-transcending love of neighbor that stems from being saved in Lutheran terms. At this point, however, one must note the paradox of grace and good works. The moment one focuses on one's own salvation in liberation activity, the project is rendered ambiguous. Grace generates spontaneous action for the neighbor. The use of liberation activity for the neighbor to gain salvation for oneself or for any other personal goal is no witness to the inner liberating action of God's grace. And, needless to say, participation in liberation movements for selfish motives can scarcely be confused with virtue of any sort, let alone the force of grace.[29]

Third, action for liberation, that is, the concrete performance of love of neighbor, is a participation in God's action in the world. The assumption here is that all genuine love of neighbor is initiated and sustained by God's liberating grace. All Christians are agreed that salvation is a work of God and of his grace, and there can be no correlation of the idea of liberation with that of salvation except insofar as it is a work of God. Here, then, human freedom is seen as a kind of instrument or agency of the movement of grace in the world. It may be added that insofar as this action for liberation is grounded solidly in the religious sphere and sustained by God's grace, it will have as its primary goal that other persons may *be* more and not simply have more.

Fourth, the primary objective of liberative action that is an effect of saving grace is the person of the neighbor; this action is a form of love of neighbor. Insofar as the neighbor is a victim of social or institutionalized oppression or violence, one must, in order to be of any real and permanent assistance, strike at the roots and causes of this objective situation. But such an action is positive; its goal is exactly the same as that of the good Samaritan, namely helping the neighbor in his specific need. This point is made to offset several confusions. One concerns the theme of conflict. Christian action for liberation cannot be in its first movement and intention conflictual, that is, simply and directly aimed against persons. It is not an overcoming of formal sin except in the self. It attacks social sin, but not in its formal or subjective aspect because Christians ought not accuse other persons of formal sin or make them thier mortal enemies. Rather, liberative action in the Christian view should address structures and institutions precisely as such, insofar as they appear objective and cause harm to other persons. These are the *effects* of sin, perhaps even in a formal sense, but they are not necessarily formal sin, that is, a function of a conscious intention and responsible freedom on the part of many who are involved. This conclusion has many practical consequences for the attitudes and rhetoric of the liberationist interpretation of Christianity.

Again, *all* institutions are ambiguous. Precisely because situations are based on general laws and common patterns of behavior, the most just society cannot be equally beneficial to all. Therefore there is always and everywhere a constant need for social commitment on the part of Christians in any culture and society. Social disease will always exist and thus there will ever be a focus for active love of neighbor that is the effect of liberating and saving grace. One does not have to live in the Third World to understand the practical import of a liberationist interpretation of Christianity. The social concern that is essential and constitutive of authentic Christian faith life, therefore, will always include de facto a concern for justice.

The practical question of how best to help the neighbor, to find a solution to his oppressive situation, is not and cannot be decided by Christian revelation or theology. These are practical and even scientific questions that can be solved only by expertise and practical judgment. Grace supplies only the inner ground and source of action, its motivation, and the formal criterion of the infinite value of the human person. Ethics and practical disciplines must work out the strategies and tactics of love of neighbor. In short and a priori, therefore, Christian action for liberation in itself commits one to no ideology. One does not necessarily have to be a Marxist to love one's neighbor effectively, or to accept a liberationist interpretation of Christianity.[30]

Fifth, the building of just social structures cannot be simply equated with salvation since even in the most objectively just social order the inner sinfulness of human beings would remain.[31] Human existence will not cease being affected with concupiscence and its consequences despite objective circumstances of law, justice, order and collective affluence. In fact it seems that the greater the material affluence of a people, the greater is the temptation to sin. Here the themes of grace as both judgment and divine forgiveness and acceptance of a people or society in spite of sin are most relevant and important. On the one hand, then, the positive force and effort at fashioning just social structures for the common good are intrinsic and constitutive of Christian faith and the salvation mediated through it, so that without this dimension and concern Christian life would be inauthentic. On the other hand, one cannot identify Christian salvation with an objective social order or structure without a subjective dimension because there can be no real salvation without an inner conversion of freedom itself.

Having said this from the point of view of personal freedom and its inclination to sin, one must also insist on the way social structures shape freedom and thus are significant for inclining persons toward good or evil. Social structures and general patterns of behavior may form, educate and incline persons toward a positive valuation of justice and thus dispose individuals toward self-transcendence even as others may encourage an opposing self-centeredness. From a historical perspective, one could interpret such positive social institutions as the objectifications of habits of grace. Institutionalized patterns of valuation and action that increase the probability of loving decision in particular instances may be seen as corresponding in the public, historical and social sphere to the infused virtues that attend upon grace in Aquinas. We shall return to this basic theme below in the consideration of social grace.

Sixth, actual love of neighbor displayed in action is also an offer of grace to all who benefit from this action precisely to the extent that it is an offer of altruistic or selfless love that invites a similar response. Moreover it is a "conviction of sin" for those guilty of or responsible for the injury of others in the same way that the externalization of the message of Christ confronts sin formally and is a call to repent, a call to conversion. There is a conflictual element in the liberationist interpretation of Christianity just as there is in the Gospel. It is this note that the symbol liberation adds to development, the latter connoting a progressive amelioration without radical change. Liberation suggests change that is more radical, even discontinuity, and this is certainly applicable where grace challenges sin and appeals for conversion. On the one hand, this conflict does not apply to Christian action against other people. On the other hand, if structures are essentially injurious to people, then one should aim at radically altering them.

It would be wrong, however, if the negative and conflictual element of the Gospel and grace became exclusive and dominant as is the tendency in the Latin American liberationist interpretation of Christianity. Because of the social situation of that continent, whose social structures are viewed as radically or essentially oppressive, the word "development," which means growth within a system, has a negative and pejorative connotation, whereas liberation, which includes the idea of changing a system or structure, is a positive symbol. But since a change in any system will involve the resistance of those whom it favors, liberation involves conflict. And this element of conflict pervades the symbol in an almost exclusive way, even when liberation is correlated with salvation and the role of the Church. This is a clear instance of the particularization of a theological symbol. It seems clear that in a situation where institutional structures were essentially sound but abused, development would be a positive symbol and liberation, insofar as it meant radical change of a system, would be negative. Correlatively, on the level of Christian interpretation, one must be careful not to view grace as exclusively a force against sin; it is also a positive force of love. And Christianity is not only a prophetic religion of judgment; it is also a vehicle for the positive building in cooperation with others of graced structures in the world. It should be noted that this is not a criticism of the liberationist interpretation of Christianity insofar as it is applied to the Latin American context, but rather a criticism of one of the particularisms of that theology that is not universally applicable and should not, therefore, be affirmed in an exclusive or normative sense.

It thus appears that saving grace at work in the human personality is not and cannot be a purely personal phenomenon in any individualistic sense precisely because it liberates a person by effecting spontaneous openness to the neighbor. In this way one can see how the whole economy of grace is historical; faith, love and hope are mediated in this world through the agency of people. Not only the message of Christ, but even more fundamentally and beyond the sphere of Christianity, grace itself is mediated historically. One cannot separate the internal and personal working of grace from its visible and outward manifestations in the lives of people insofar as they affect other people. God works in the human personality and in history through the agency of human beings.

Social Grace

The grace that first of all has its effects within the personality is also social insofar as it is a force of self-transcendence. And insofar as grace becomes real and tangible in concrete human acitivity it can become institutionalized as any other human activity can. As Rahner has pointed out, the grace underlying human history does not remain merely secret but breaks through into the public sphere and often takes an organized form.[32] From the Christian point of view, the paradigmatic example of institutionalized or social grace is the Christian Church, that is, if it existed in its ideal state. But other religions are also examples of social grace and in specific concrete cases may be better historical agents of grace than the Christian Church. And, finally, since one cannot separate the history of grace from profane or secular history, one might expect examples of social grace in everyday historical existence as well. It should be noted further that secular humanism itself functions as a religion for many in our culture. More particularly, the family, insofar as it nurtures the members and fosters mutual love, might be considered a graced social pattern of existence. Other more voluntary organizations dedicated to the welfare of others, such as a hospital or Alcoholics Anonymous, may be institutionalized forms of love and are therefore social grace.

This shift of focus from the personal to the public, historical level of understanding, and the use of the concept of "social grace," entails a double movement or dynamism to God's action in history. This may be seen in a simultaneous inward and upward movement on the one hand, and on the other an external and downward movement, both, however, always within history itself. The inward liberating grace experienced by people, both by individuals and within groups, externalizes itself and moves upward so to speak in a process of objectification. It becomes institutionalized. At the same time, those institutions influence others, especially those who are socialized into them. Not only the ritual patterns of worship and the linguistic world of doctrine, but also the language and social patterns of care and concern and service of others, may be regarded as external grace for the world. In this way, the action of God in history through grace may be seen as an objective movement that ultimately rests on the stuff of graced human freedom(s), but that at the same time enjoys an objective social and public visibility. It is true that an exclusive emphasis on this objective and organizational side of the dynamism of grace could lead to repressive social action in the name of God (as in the case of Augustine with the Donatists). But a moment's reflection on such policy is enough to reveal that coercive action or repressive social and political structures are by their very nature a contradiction of a grace that both externally appeals to freedom and internally liberates it.

Just as social sin is a complex and nuanced, indeed a paradoxical, concept, so too is social grace. Insofar as an organization becomes objectified and routinized it may lack precisely the spontaneity and self-actualized intention of self-transcending love that is the fruit of grace. The original intention and motive and direction may be lost.[33] Moreover, there are probably no examples of pure social grace any more than there are of pure social sin. And still another caution must be introduced. No theology of grace, and consequently no Christian view of history, can fail to recognize the tragic side of the human enterprise. The Cross of Christ is the permanent Christian symbol of the ever-present and all-pervasive reality of sin. This sin is located in the human spirit itself, collectively and in each person; it is rooted within human freedom itself; and therefore it is part of the very stuff of history. Thus no human structure that serves to release the human spirit in freedom can ensure that the exercise of that freedom will not be sinful. Two consequences flow from this, the one objective and the other subjective. Objectively, it is impossible to affirm a progressivist evolutionary view of the history of grace because of the constant presence of sin within human freedom. And subjectively, a spirituality whose inner life is animated by a desire to participate in God's action in history must include within itself the possibility if not the necessity of personal failure in this world if it is not to run headlong into disillusionment.

The Goal of History

Having said that, however, we may still ask about the goal of history in a penultimate sense. Granted that ultimate or final salvation is to be realized outside of history in the Christian vision, and granted the stark reality of sin, still one may inquire as to the goal of history *in this world* on the supposition that this goal cannot be considered as completely discontinuous with the former. May we not say that the goal or purpose of grace in this world is to build more and more institutions that incarnate, mediate and foster in the world the effects of grace, namely, forgiveness, self-transcending love, communities of reconciliation and concern? And if this is the case, is not this also an expression of the goal of history under the influence of grace?

To say that the kingdom of God is the goal of the history of this world is not to assert that this goal will or can be achieved, at least by human beings. For history is not nature, but a function of human freedom, and that freedom is marked by sin. The future is open and uncertain, except that it will certainly not exclude sin. To say that the kingdom of God is the goal of this our history in time, therefore, is to make a religious statement. Like "utopia," it is a proposition that both judges the contemporary situation and draws forth creative energies for the future. It is an affirmation of a hope that is based on faith, a hope in something that manifestly exceeds human possibility. And yet it is a conviction that generates a desire to make one's own life an agent of God's possibility.

This view is not inconsistent with certain themes in the tradition of the theology of grace especially as seen in Aquinas and Augustine. If one interprets Aquinas from within a context of a consciousness of history, that is, by shifting his teleological understanding of human nature into a historical and eschatological context, one can say that God's action in and through human loving by cooperative grace is moving toward the goal of his kingdom, the kingdom of communion, harmony, peace, reconciliation. This goal is not totally discontinuous with history but is realized in it and through it. Therefore the limited but real goal of God's grace in and for history is that grace become more and more the substance and ground of historical and cultural institutions. Grace is thus God's action in history, through human freedom, tending toward the fulfillment of his own designs in history.

Conclusion

As a conclusion, four observations may be made concerning a liberationist theology of grace. The first is that one cannot separate the sphere of so-called secular history from the sphere of the operation of grace. There is but one history and the whole of it is supported by and under the influence of the immanent working of God through his grace. Wherever there is self-transcendence and altruism, in whatever form, there one can find the working of grace.

Second, whereas the direct saving action of God's grace is experienced within personal freedom, once the context is shifted to the interpersonal and social levels, one must also attend to the objective consequences of self-transcending action toward others. "Love and do what you will" attends to personal salvation, but not to the effects of graced human behavior within interpersonal or social contexts. We have only considered in this final chapter a first stage of a theory of social grace, namely, the grounding of such a concept. In order for it to be operative there must be research into the kind of altruistic behavior required in a given situation. What forms of graced action should be institutionalized? What will be the effects of this or that institution or social policy? These are questions that require study by the human sciences and Christian ethics and responses must be consonant with the particularities of circumstance. Once one admits a concept of social grace, one that is objective and external, then one must also look carefully at the objective consequences of social behavior.

Third, this view of grace should provide the basis for a spirituality that is both modern and genuinely Christian. It would be a spirituality that sees the operation of grace made manifest precisely in a "building of the earth" in history, among people, in public institutions that shape human lives. As such, this spirituality would be the very opposite of one that called for a withdrawal from the "world," from secular and profane activities. For this spirituality would see grace as a call to participate in history. This Christian spirituality would entail an immersion in the processes of history; in the public events and crises, large and small, that influence other lives in this world; in the corporate institutions and structures that shape and govern human existence in the world; in the small or local institutions or ways of life that often oppress and dehumanize this group or render that one powerless and passive. In this spirituality the idea of "saintliness" could not consist in a "state of life," but would only apply existentially and concretely to some form of engaged behavior.

Not only would there be no double standard of Christian "perfection"; the natural tendency to predicate perfection to a life of detachment, withdrawal and contemplation over against an active life in the world would be simply reversed. Monastic life, although it may be justified as a particular way of life, could in no way appear as standard or ideal.

Finally, this view of history and its consequent spirituality may be seen as fundamentally in line with the Christian understanding of grace. One must not view God and the human person in competition. God works within and guarantees human autonomy and its ability to transcend itself. From a merely human point of view, then, the goals of history laid down here are goals that strictly transcend human capabilities. But in Aquinas's terms, grace is precisely needed to accomplish that which transcends the finite and limited powers of human nature. There can be no correlation between liberation and grace unless liberation is seen as the work of grace, for Christians are all agreed that saving liberation is God's work and not that of human beings. But if one recalls that grace works through human freedom and not independent of human response and action, then there is no need to fear Pelagianism. In the words of Rahner:

When the basic relationship between God and the world is correctly viewed, excluding any anthropomorphic "synergism," the action of God appears as the possibility and dynamism of the action of the world, which moves in self-transcendence to its fulfillment. . . . World history may well be regarded as humanity's self-liberation from self-alienation. History in this sense takes place in moral action made possible by God's action, as a moment of rightly understood self-redemption of man, given to mankind as its task.[34]

Notes

1. Karl Rahner, "The Mission of the Church and the Humanizing of the World," *Doctrine and Life*, (April 1971), pp. 174–178.

2. An objective theological theory and systematic conceptualization of God's nature and how he has effected Redemption objectively is the term of

theological understanding and not its point of departure. Given the post-enlightenment situation of modern theology one cannot begin one's theological understanding from a preformed objective theory.

3. The principle of inculturation involves a tension between the universal and its particular manifestations and requires a nuanced interpretation of what is essential and normative in Christian faith experience as distinguishable from its explicit expression in cultural forms. Just as Christians of former mission areas were asked to inculturate Western Christianity into their local situations, so now it seems that Western Christianity is beginning to be asked to receive back and adapt into Western traditions insights gained in the Third World.

4. "Distinction" does not mean "separation"; there can be no expression of pure Christian faith outside of a culturally relative human focus.

5. "Essential" and "constitutive" mean that if this dimension is lacking, Christian faith life is inauthentic, as is implied by the famous sentence of the 1971 Roman Catholic Bishops Synod: "Action on behalf of justice and participation in the transformation of the world fully appear to us as a constitutive dimension of the preaching of the Gospel, or, in other words, of the Church's mission for the redemption of the human race and its liberation from every oppressive situation" (1971 Synod of Bishops, *Justice in the World*, Introduction).

6. See, for example, Gustavo Gutierrez, *A Theology of Liberation* (Maryknoll, N.Y.: Orbis Books, 1973), pp. 33–37, 175–178.

7. In the liberation theology of Juan Luis Segundo the theology of grace plays a major role. See his *Grace and the Human Condition* (Maryknoll, N.Y.: Orbis Books, 1973) in relation to the five-volume work *Theology for Artisans of a New Humanity* (Maryknoll, N.Y.: Orbis Books, 1973–1975) of which it is a part.

8. See Ruben A. Alves, *A Theology of Human Hope* (New York: Corpus Books, 1963), pp. 87ff.

9. This can be seen in terms of the principle of sacramentality, which maintains that human beings in this world can encounter God only through this world of concrete symbols and events. This need not be radically contrasted to a prophetic Word tradition of understanding grace and salvation since ultimately "word" is also a human symbol and needs mediation. See Franz Leenhardt, "This is My Body," in *Essays on the Lord's Supper*, ed. O. Cullmann and F. Leenhardt (Richmond: John Knox Press, 1958), p. 35.

10. This is not to deny that ultimately such theories are necessary for systematic theology. They should, however, conform to concrete historical data and a consistent anthropology and cosmology.

11. Thus the terms "world" and "sin" are not synonymous terms and need not necessarily be correlated.

12. See Karl Rahner, "Concerning the Relationship between Nature and Grace," *Theological Investigations* I (Baltimore: Helicon Press, 1961), pp. 297–317. Also relevant are his articles "Nature and Grace," *Theological Investigations* IV (Baltimore: Helicon Press, 1966), pp. 165–188, and "The

Order of Redemption within the Order of Creation," *The Christian Commitment* (New York: Sheed and Ward, 1963), pp. 38–74.

13. See Karl Rahner, "History of the World and Salvation History," *Theological Investigations* V, pp. 97–114. While this may seem an unduly positive view of history, it is so only from the point of view of Christian *faith* in God. This same history is also one of human irresponsibility, sin and guilt so that such a view of history can only be one of faith.

14. Ibid., pp. 98–99.

15. Ibid., p. 98.

16. Karl Rahner, "Salvation," *Sacramentum Mundi* V (New York: Herder and Herder, 1970), p. 430.

17. For a clear example of where Augustine presents God acting in history through his influence on human subjects by his election and grace see his *Grace and Free Will*, chap. XLI–XLIII, *Basic Writings of Saint Augustine*, I, ed. Whitney J. Oates (New York: Random House, 1948), pp. 767–771.

18. For the division (or, better, distinction, for it is the same grace) between operative and cooperative grace. *ST*, I–II, q. 111, a. 2; for the effects of operative grace, namely justification, q. 113; and for the effects of cooperative grace, namely "merit," q. 114. The category of cooperative grace (and by implicit contrast operative or sheerly prevenient grace) is also found in Augustine's anti-Pelagian writings.

19. Substantially the same view appears in Augustine where he maintains that grace does not destroy freedom but sustains it while at the same time loving freedom is a consent to the power and movement of grace. *On the Spirit and the Letter*, chap. LX, *Basic Writings of Saint Augustine*, p. 512.

20. Cf. Chapter 1, pp. 20–22.

21. William James, *The Varieties of Religious Experience* (New York: Collier Books, 1961), p. 285.

22. Eugene TeSelle, "The Problem of Nature and Grace," *The Journal of Religion* 45 (1965): 238–241. See Chapter 3, pp. 74–75.

23. Brian Gerrish, *Grace and Reason: A Study of the Theology of Luther* (Oxford: Clarendon Press, 1962), pp. 131–133.

24. This may be done because the methods and conclusions of Luther over against those of either Aquinas or Trent are not contradictory despite the language of the canons of the *Decree on Justification*. Scholastic suppositions underlie this Tridentine statement, despite its Scriptural phrasing and, as Otto Pesch has shown, the basis or gound of understanding, the method and consequently the meaning, of Luther and Scholasticism is not contradictory but simply different because assertions are made from different points of view. See Otto Pesch, *art. cit.* It might be added that Calvin's introduction of the distinction between justification and sanctification meets this problem squarely and at the same time retains the Reformation's emphasis on the divine initiative with respect to justification. See Chapter 5, pp. 94–96, for a fuller explanation of contrasting Thomistic and Lutheran spiritualities.

25. One could of course define sin objectively and mean human action that is against God's will whether the actor is aware of it or not. In this usage, however, the concepts of "evil" and "sin" tend to merge and on the level of social sin this causes enormous confusions. Moreover, even if one imagined a perfect society with objectively just social structures and material well being, sin in its deepest sense would remain, for it is part of the existential human condition. Ultimately, one must resist the temptation to completely objectify both sin and salvation..

26. Peter Berger, *The Social Construction of Reality: A Treatise in the Sociology of Knowledge* (Garden City, N.Y.: Anchor Books, Doubleday, 1967), pp. 60–61.

27. Personal sin, too, must be disclosed to a person, for how else could people know they could be other or more than they are? Grace then is also revelatory, for it discloses to humanity that the way things are is not so necessarily and can ultimately be different.

28. This is an ontological statement. In a chronological sense grace is mediated to any individual through a community so that one may wish to view the objective means of grace in a community as prior to its operation in any given person. Such a view, however, should be seen as practical and functional. Logically, persons are prior to community. And ontologically, although the individual and the community exist in a mutually causative relation, one should avoid the tendency that flows from this insight to reify community.

29. Here one sees that the judgment of intentions, the question of formal sin, works both ways. For this reason the term "sin" is a highly volatile and often counterproductive category in public rhetoric. It often confuses justice with subjective virtue, and thereby projects a superior moral attitude. In its public discourse (as opposed to its theology) liberation movements would be more effective arguing toward objective justice against objective injustice rather than against sin.

30. It may be, of course, that in this or that historical situation a Marxist analysis is appropriate and should provide the theoretical basis for the most effective practice of love of neighbor.

31. This point is made forcefully by Langdon Gilkey in his new book *Reaping the Whirlwind* (New York: Seabury Press, 1976), pp. 236–237.

32. Rahner, "History of the World and Salvation History," pp. 99–100. See also Karl Rahner, "Christianity and the Non-Christian Religions," *Theological Investigations* V, pp. 125–131.

33. Moreover, dehumanizing activity might be the actual reality inside the outer form and contrary to its primary intention. Modern hospitals are often a good example of this.

34. Karl Rahner, "Salvation," *Sacramentum Mundi* V, p. 437.